DI006277

IT'S UP TO US

Ten Little Ways We Can Bring About Big Change

Also by John Kasich

Courage Is Contagious
Stand for Something
Every Other Monday
Two Paths

JOHN KASICH

WITH DANIEL PAISNER

IT'S UP TO US

TO US

Ten Little Ways We Can Bring About Big Change

HANOVER
SQUARE
PRESS

HANOVER
SQUARE
PRESS

ISBN-13: 978-1-335-01220-3

It's Up to Us: Ten Little Ways We Can Bring About Big Change

For questions and comments about the quality of this book, please contact us at CustomerService@Harlequin.com.

Library of Congress Cataloging-in-Publication Data has been applied for.

HanoverSqPress.com
BookClubbish.com

Printed in U.S.A.

To everyone who is working to change the world.

Contents

Each time a man stands up for an ideal, or acts to improve the lot of others, or strikes out against injustice, he sends forth a tiny ripple of hope, and crossing each other from a million different centers of energy and daring those ripples build a current which can sweep down the mightiest walls of oppression and resistance.

—Robert F. Kennedy

Introduction

Nothing Good Is Lost

If I cannot do great things, I can do small things in a great way.

—Martin Luther King, Jr.

Why is it that in the run-up to every national election we're told that it's going to be the most important election in American history? Politicians, pundits, journalists…they're all out there saying pretty much the same thing, over and over, but it never turns out to be the case.

What happens when the elections are over? It's "meet the new boss, same as the old boss." If you can't place the reference, that's a classic rock lyric from The Who's "Won't Get Fooled Again," but the title is where they lose me, because most of us get fooled every single time. We do. We allow ourselves to be whipped into some kind of frenzy by the media and the moment, to the point where we're made to think our future hangs on the outcome of this or that election, only to find out that the world continues to spin on its axis. We catch our breath and return to our days, loving our families, worshipping our God, grousing about something the president did or said or tweeted, and doing our best to make the world a little bit better for our being here.

Sure, our elections are important—but some elections matter more than others. Our presidential elections perhaps matter most of all because when we elect a president we look to him or her to be a leader for all of America. The president helps to set a national tone and shape our national conversation. The tone can be inclusive, supportive, and aspirational, or it can be negative, divisive, and incendiary. The conversation can lift us up or drive us down. But ultimately, it's on us to embrace that tone or reject it, to continue the conversation or set it aside in favor of a new one.

Don't misunderstand me: the office of the presidency is arguably the most powerful position on the planet—and it's certainly the most influential. The president can take us to war. He or she can adopt policies on immigration, health care, the environment, and a host of other issues that can profoundly impact our lives for a generation. Of course, for most of these changes a president would have to go through Congress. He or she could also use executive authority to bring about change, or make judicial appointments, but even here that power would have to be ratified, either by Congress or the courts.

The point I want to make here at the outset is that we shouldn't be investing all of our emotions in that one office in the White House. Instead, we ought to be looking to our own houses, our own communities, and spending some time thinking about what we can do, together with our friends and family, to set the right tone for this nation, and to set us on the right path.

When I ran for president in 2016, I believed I could make a difference and set a positive example, but as I stepped away from the race I started to realize what I must have known on some level all along: even though it matters who sits in the White House, it doesn't matter as much as *we* matter. The power of the presidency should not obscure or discount the power of the people. Each of us has the ability to make as much of an impact in our communities as the president is able to make on a national or international scale. As a nation of caring, thinking, *feeling* people, we are not powerless in the grand scheme of our democracy; in fact, we can be profoundly powerful in small ways that can have an enormous impact on the lives all around us.

All of which takes me to the central thesis of these pages: what you do matters. What *we* do matters. We are blessed with the ability to make a difference, to send a message to the powerful elites in Washington, to put it out there that the change we want to see is the change we're prepared to make happen.

Think about some of the great changes that have taken place in this country over the past 250 years. Think about some of the ways we've moved the needle on progress and tolerance and opportunity. Most of the time, these changes have come about at the ground level. Societal change flows from the bottom up, and not from the top down, and it's almost always driven by the passion and purpose of selfless individuals who push for a way to make these changes happen—they demand them, *really*, and it doesn't matter who's sitting in office when the voices of the people have something to say.

Think about this, too: on a day-to-day basis, does the president truly affect you? Here again, not as much as most people think. Absolutely, the president can make a kind of statement about who we are on the world stage; for good or ill, he or she becomes the public face of our great nation. But I'll tell you what *really* affects you: your family, your neighbors, your community, the road that needs repaving on the way into town, or the new turf field the booster club is hoping to lay in over at the high school so your student-athletes can practice in all kinds of weather.

What matters is how we do right by each other, how we collaborate with our coworkers, how we show kindness to those in need, and how we receive kindness in return. It matters how we make room in our lives for faith and family and friendships. I want to spend some time on these things in the pages ahead because I believe they are important. In fact, I believe they are *all-important*. Why does my opinion matter? Well, I have some experience in this area. I've served in public office for thirty years, including nine terms as an Ohio congressman and two terms as Ohio's governor. I've run for president. Twice. I've got a pretty good idea how our government works at all levels, and how it doesn't, and now that I'm out here in the private sector I'd like to think I've learned a thing or two about how to contribute in a meaningful way to our American conversation.

By the way, a lot of people don't remember that I ran for president in 2000, and the reason they don't remember is because I didn't get very far. I didn't have a whole lot of name recognition back then, and I couldn't raise a whole lot of money, so I left the race almost as soon as I entered it. I got a little bit farther in 2016, when I joined a pack of seventeen hopefuls seeking the Republican nomination—again, without a whole lot of name recognition or money, but this time I managed to hang in there long enough to be the last Republican standing against our eventual nominee.

What I discovered on the campaign trail—or, I should say, what I *rediscovered* as I met hundreds of thousands of people all across the country—was that our American ideal is very much alive in this country, and that the American heartland is very aptly named. America has a big heart. It's a land of hope and plenty, where our shared values are mostly in sync, and where there are opportunities all around. Politicians can talk all they want about policy and programs, and political analysts can talk about the issues that divide us, but what the American people care about are the ways they can come together. They want to know that their elected officials *hear* them…that they *see* them…that they *get* them.

I did.

And, now, I still do.

The American people want to make a difference

where they work and live, and here in this book I mean to shine a light on the ways we can move this country forward. Together. Without waiting for a push or for permission from Washington. It doesn't take a lot, when you break it down. Mostly, it takes stepping away from our workaday worries and setting aside our differences and recognizing that we need to live a life bigger than ourselves. We need to show up for the people in our lives, for the people in our communities. We need to stand and be counted. And we need to understand that it's on each and every one of us to bring about the changes we seek. That's a pretty powerful concept, don't you think? To embrace the notion that there's no silver bullet or magic potion for what ails America, and to accept responsibility for the America to come.

There is only us.

As powerful concepts go, this one's also powerfully simple, and absolutely within reach. All it takes, really, is a commitment to each other that we can do better by each other—that we *must* do better by each other.

And, that the time to start doing better by each other is now.

With this book, I'm hoping to jump-start a new conversation, one in which we stop throwing up our hands and worrying over who sits in the White House, or who's going to lead our party, and instead start sharing ideas on the best ways to develop our personal power. Just how am I going to do that? Well, maybe it's better to tell you how I'm *not* going to do that. I'm not going to shout or point fingers. I'm not going to bash the president. I'm not going to highlight the deep divisions that exist in this country, or call out any of our elected officials or political commentators who sometimes seem to want to deepen those divisions. If that's what you're looking for, you should probably look somewhere else.

One thing you should know about me as we start in on this enterprise: I'm a collector of stories that illustrate the ways we can lift each other up. I'm always on the lookout for examples of people living a life bigger than themselves. I collect these stories because they inspire me, excite me, and affirm for me the goodness of the human spirit. They remind me, yet again and each time out, that anything is possible—indeed, that *everything* is possible. I'm hoping they do the same for you, and I'll share a few of them here to highlight some of the general themes we're about to consider.

Let's start with the story of a child I spoke to back when I was still governor—a five-year-old girl from

Chicago named Florence Wisniewski, who got it in her head in the summer of 2018 to help the people of North and South Carolina whose lives had been devastated by the killing winds and tidal flooding of Hurricane Florence. Little Flo hated to see the pictures on the news of so many people suffering, and she also hated that all of that suffering was somehow connected to her name. She was embarrassed a little bit, thought maybe her friends would think she was bad, but even more than that she was heartbroken.

So what did she do? She turned to her mother and said, "Mom, these people are gonna need Band-Aids." That was how she'd processed what was going on in the Carolinas—isn't that something? At just five years old, this child saw a basic need and decided it was up to her to try and fill it, so she recruited her little brother and the two of them went around the neighborhood, pulling a red wagon and asking people to donate first aid supplies. How she corralled her brother into this, I can't begin to imagine, but they ended up filling an entire garage—not *just* with Band-Aids, but with diapers and toys and cleaning supplies and anything else their neighbors thought people might need. Flo created her own movement and persuaded all these good people to sign on to it.

She had some help in this, of course. Flo's mother arranged for a local ministry to assist with the delivery of supplies, and when I heard about this story I made a special point to reach out and let this little girl with the big heart know how important she was, how special. I spoke to her mother—because, after all, no five-year-old girl wants to get on the phone to talk to the governor of Ohio, right?—and I told her that she, too, was special to have raised a daughter who was moved in this way.

Flo's mother said something I thought was pretty interesting. She said she didn't see Flo's mission as an act of charity. "It's really just common sense," she said.

Common sense. We don't seem to be seeing or hearing a whole lot of that from some of our leaders these days, and I'm afraid it's hard to recognize in the din of commentary on social media and some of our national news outlets, but it's out there in full force. We just need to look for it, to listen for it, to find it in ourselves and tap in to it—and if we don't see it in our leaders, we ought to do something about it.

Now, before you start wondering just how you might do something about it, I've got another story to share. I opened the newspaper one day this past winter and read about a Toronto rabbi who was concerned that a Holocaust survivor he was visiting in the hospital would not receive a proper Jewish burial. The survivor's name was Eddie Ford, and he'd once sang in the choir of the largest synagogue in Europe. Mr. Ford had been sheltered during the war by a Christian family and had lost touch with his Jewish roots. By the age of eighty-five, in failing health, his only connection to the faith of his childhood were the melodies that accompanied the prayers he used to chant in the choir.

Custom holds that a Jewish burial be conducted in the presence of a *minyan*—ten adult Jews who join in all ritual acts of prayer. The idea behind this kind of quorum is that a prayer will not be heard unless it is lifted by ten voices—a reminder to all of the strength we find in community. Mr. Ford was fairly alone in this world, and the few friends and aides who might have shown up to his funeral to pay their respects were not Jewish, so this volunteer rabbi posted something on Facebook when Mr. Ford finally passed, putting out the call that a *minyan* was needed for the funeral of a Holocaust survivor.

Understand, it is considered a good deed for a Jew to stand and be counted in prayer. Understand, too, that temperatures were below zero at the cemetery north of Toronto where the graveside service was being held—-14 Celsius, or -23 Celsius with the windchill—so this was one of those times where custom and circumstance might have been at odds.

(Hey, good deeds are hard to come by in the freezing cold.)

As the rabbi drove to the cemetery he worried there would not be enough people to say the traditional Jewish prayer of mourning. When he arrived he saw a long line of parked cars, and a crowd of a couple hundred people, and he wondered for a moment who else was being buried on this day. He'd never seen such a long line of cars. Whomever it was must have lived a big, full life, because this was really quite a turnout. But the turnout was for Mr. Ford, a complete stranger to these bighearted people, who had braved the weather and upended their day to lend their voices in prayer and help to bury a man they never knew.

The great lesson here: sometimes in life all you have to do is show up. That's all.

Did this rabbi in Toronto change the world? Did those couple hundred mourners who took the time to stand in memory of Mr. Ford? Are you kidding me? What about that little girl, Flo? Did she change the world? You don't really need me to answer that, do you?

We change the world in ways big and small. We change the world by doing for others, by showing up for others…even for folks we'll never meet. We change the world by living our lives as an example—that's probably the best legacy we can hope to leave, don't you think? Anyway, it's the only one we can really count on, the only one that's entirely within our control. You see, after a lifetime in politics, I've come to a realization: no one really remembers you once you leave office. There are exceptions to this, of course—we name schools and airports after our former presidents, and at the local level we put up plaques to honor former mayors and town councilpersons. But most elected officials slip quietly into the background once they leave public life. After leaving Congress, I used to joke that there was no longer any reason for me to have a phone, because no one was calling me and no one would take my calls, and I repeat the joke here to say that you shouldn't seek public office *just* to get the important people in your community to take your calls or seek you out for your support or opinion on an issue.

We shouldn't devote our lives to public service hoping or expecting to be recognized for that devotion. No, we should do it to answer some kind of call, because we feel we have something to contribute to the conversation, some special skill set or talent that could help to make our town, our city, our state, our nation a better place. But as I hope this book will make clear, running for office isn't the *only* way to bring about meaningful change. In fact, it might not even be the *best* way. No, for that we must look inward, and we must look next door. We must look to the ways we carry ourselves, and to the ways we might lift someone else on the back of a simple kindness or on the strength of a powerful idea.

We must look to the hostess at a Chuck E. Cheese's restaurant in Queens, who went out of her way to give one of her regular customers a hug—no big thing, until you hear the rest of the story. You see, there was a New York City photographer who was in the habit of taking his autistic son, Billy, to Chuck E. Cheese's every Sunday afternoon. For years, Billy would remind his father to be at the restaurant at 3:30 p.m. because that was when Chuck E. Cheese himself made an appearance. The costumed mouse worked the room for twenty minutes or so, signing autographs, posing for pictures, dispensing hugs. Billy was a great fan of hugs, so he was always first in line.

One Sunday, there was a ton of traffic and Billy and his dad arrived at about 3:50 p.m., after Chuck E. had come and gone. The photographer knew Billy would be inconsolable if he missed his hug so he flagged down this young hostess. She already knew Billy—in fact, the entire staff was always sweet and welcoming. The photographer quietly explained that Billy was prone to tantrums when he was separated from his routines. This is how it is for a lot of families with a child on the spectrum, only in Billy's case, at twenty years old and over two hundred pounds, his "tantrums" could get a little unwieldy. The hostess said she'd check the break room to see if the guy who played Chuck E. was still in costume, while Billy went around the restaurant hugging the other customers and employees. After about five minutes, the young woman came back out…wearing the Chuck E. Cheese costume! The regular Chuck E. had gone home for the day, so she put on the costume herself, just so Billy could have his hug. The costume was a couple sizes too big, but to Billy and his dad it was just right.

Did this young woman change the world? You better believe it. On this one Sunday afternoon, at this one restaurant in Queens, she made all the difference in the lives of this young autistic man and his father. She lit up their day, and the way she did it was simple. She showed up. She made an extra effort, and if it happens that the extra efforts you're inspired to make lead you to a life of public service...well, then that's great. If they don't...well, then, that's great, too, because it's on each of us to serve in our own way.

As I write this, I note the sad passing of a man named Jim Nicholson. I'm betting most readers have never heard of him, but he was one of the finest obituary writers in the country—one of the first to shine meaningful light on the lives of ordinary citizens. He wrote for several newspapers in his long career, including the *Philadelphia Daily News*, and he was known for his tributes to average, hardworking Americans who helped to enrich their communities in ways big and small. He chose his subjects based on the impact they'd had on those closest to them, and people really responded to the stories he shared. He was honored with a lifetime achievement award by the Society of Professional Obituary Writers. It's because of Jim's influence that you'll likely find an obit for your two-term state senator alongside one for a local florist, say, who donated bridal bouquets to veterans and children of veterans.

I hadn't heard of Jim Nicholson either until I read about his death and recognized the *essentialness* of his life's work, celebrating the *essentialness* of the "nobodies" in our communities, as he called them. I was struck by a line from his own obit—a question he often asked in response to people who questioned his decision to devote his career to writing these under-the-radar, out-of-the-way obituaries: "Who would you miss more when he goes on vacation, the secretary of state or your garbage man?"

I read that line and thought immediately of my father. Before I tell you why, I should probably set the scene. I grew up in a small town outside of Pittsburgh called McKees Rocks. My father carried mail on his back. His father was a coal miner. My mother also worked, depending on what stage of life we kids were in. On each side of my family tree there was this sense that nothing was ever handed to you, and that nothing good was lost. The abiding lesson was to work hard and to make time for others. Success in our house was measured in what we were able to do for each other and not in what we were able to do for ourselves, and the values I took in from my parents probably look a lot like the values most people carry: personal responsibility, honesty, integrity, humility, faith, charity.

One thing I want to emphasize here is that even though these values were very much in place in and around our household, in and around McKees Rocks, I didn't always hold to them. They were something to aspire to, a moral compass I was meant to follow, but I was a little all over the place when I was a kid—and, frankly, I'm still wide of the mark when I try to live up to the model my parents set for me. Nevertheless, I was taught to do the right thing—and, just as important, to know how to recognize the right thing. Let's face it, we all fail from time to time. Some fail more than most, but we all fall short every now and then, so I don't want to come across as a hypocrite here. I struggle with some of this stuff, I do. I don't always treat people the way they deserve to be treated, especially now when I'm being recognized more and more as I travel the country. People stop me in airports, or when I go down to the hotel restaurant in the lobby to get a bite to eat. Maybe they just want to say hello, or shake my hand, or take a picture with me, and most of the time I'm happy for the exchange, but there are a lot of times when I'm tired and grumpy and not the

most gracious person in the world. I try not to beat
myself up over this, because I'm human, same as you.
Whatever goals we set for ourselves, whatever virtues
we mean to uphold, we're bound to miss a couple, but
the true test comes when we fail or misstep—in the
ways we motivate ourselves to try again tomorrow.

The reason I thought of my father when I read that
line from the obituary writer was that he made time
for people. He knew everybody on his mail route. He
knew what was going on with their families. He was
a fixture in their lives, same way they were a fixture
in his, and in this small, sure way he was as integral to
their days as the president, the governor of our state,
or the mayor of our small town. This is not a knock
on any of those elected officials, or a false assessment
of my father…no, it's just how it was. The folks on
my father's mail route looked forward to his visits
each day. Sure, they liked receiving their mail, but
it was more than that. They liked the way he asked
after their children, or took the time to notice that
the azalea bushes were coming in nicely that year or
that the shutters had been repainted.

What a lot of people find interesting when they hear
my story is the fact that I was raised in a Democratic
household. I don't think I met a Republican until I

went away to college—it's like they had roadblocks set up to keep them out of McKees Rocks. That line always gets a laugh when I share it with an audience, but it's the truth, except for the part about the roadblocks. Ours was a hardworking, blue-collar household, in what was for the most part a hardworking, blue-collar town. Everyone kind of looked after each other, and expected a lot from each other. Sadly, that feeling of connectedness is missing in many of our communities these days. What's also missing is room in our public discourse for an alternative point of view, and in our house, once I started paying attention to the ways the world worked (and, to some of the ways it didn't), that alternative point of view was often coming from me. It didn't change anything between us if we disagreed from time to time. We were all coming from the same place. We all cared for each other, and wanted the best for each other, and our difference of opinion on how to achieve the best for each other was just one of the ways we cared for each other.

We had our own ideas, while still holding fast to a shared set of ideals, and even when we differed on a policy or approach we would take the time to listen to someone else's idea, and if it made more sense than our own we found a way to attach it to our worldview.

By the way, over time my mother became a little more conservative than my father. She even registered as a Republican, but what I've always thought was remarkable—then and still—was the way there was room under our roof for differences of opinion. I've written about these things before, and talked about them at town halls all across the country during the 2016 presidential race, but I offer them again here to underline the ideas I mean to share about how to bridge the deepening divide in America today.

You see, I'm troubled by the ways we appear to be at odds with each other.

I'm troubled at how so many of us seem to hold fast to our narrow points of view, without making room in our thinking for different perspectives.

I'm troubled by the general impression I get from a lot of folks that the best days of our lives as individuals and the best days of our lives as a nation are somehow behind us.

But I'm here to tell you that the best of America is yet to come. I firmly believe this. And I also believe that it's on each of us to do our part to help to make this happen. Those values we all share? They're part of the fabric of this nation. We can't expect our leaders in Washington to turn things around for us, and

I'm afraid our local officials don't always have our backs on this either. In fact, I've been thinking a lot these days about how we can all take on leadership roles in our own lives and communities because the strength and resilience of our nation lies in each of us, as individuals. We are all leaders to someone, or to some group, and we cannot take that responsibility lightly. That's what this book is about, at bottom—the ways we might reestablish a hopeful, helpful tone in our national conversation and return our attention to the families and communities at the heart of our America.

It's about the little things we can do to make a big difference in the lives of the people around us.

It's about believing in something bigger than ourselves.

It's about doing the right thing. Think about it: we all know what it is to do the right thing—it's written on our hearts, just as it was written on mine as a small boy in McKees Rocks, and once we understand that we're all cut in mostly the same ways on this, once we allow our values to guide us, it's easy to find our true north.

The small acts of kindness I've shared here remind us that everything we do accrues to the good—and, inversely, that everything we *don't* do lines up against us. The hostess who put on her colleague's Chuck E. Cheese costume just to collect a hug from the autistic man who could not be shaken from his routines? That meant the world to this young man and his father. It took this caring person just five minutes to make a meaningful difference in the lives of two people she only knew to smile at every Sunday. How many people do you know who would have taken it on themselves to do the same thing? What about you—would *you* have donned that costume to brighten one person's day? I've got to be honest here: I'm not so sure it would have even occurred to me to do something like this if I had been in the hostess's position, so it really is kind of remarkable that she gave of herself in this sweet, selfless way. It wasn't expected of her, but the fact that she had this notion *and* the strength of character to act on it was an astonishing thing. And the thing of it is, if she *hadn't* acted on it...well, our world would be a slightly darker place.

Those mourners who braved the cold to join in prayer and help to bury a man who was alone in this world and alone in his faith? Same deal: it didn't take a whole lot for these folks to carve a few minutes from their day, but those few minutes made a lasting difference. The good stuff adds up and here I hope to shine a light on some of the ways we can do good, some of the ways we can do *better*, because every little thing counts. Every small kindness, every generous gesture, every moment of care and intention…it all adds up.

Look, we all want the same things. We want to live a life of purpose and meaning. We want to leave some kind of legacy for our children and grandchildren. We want to leave the world a better place. And yet too many of us spend too much time wringing our hands over what's wrong in our country, and not nearly enough time on the ways we might make things right. We talk more about the issues that separate us than we do about what brings us together. We talk about what's broken instead of what's working beautifully. We size each other up, and position ourselves on the left, or on the right, or somewhere in the middle, and the conversation becomes more about where we stand than what it is we stand for, but that just doesn't cut it if we hope to fill the spaces between us and move forward.

Just how are we going to do that? Well, I have some ideas—ten of them, in fact. *Ten little ways we can bring about big change.* That's what it says on the cover, but

I'm not out to spin a bunch of political bromides or wax nostalgic about the death of civility in our culture. I'm not suggesting that holding the door open for the person behind you or returning your shopping cart from the supermarket parking lot is going to solve America's problems—although, frankly, we ought to be doing more of that type of thing. And I'm certainly not looking to write some saccharine treatise about the ways we can treat each other more decently, more purposefully—although we can do with more of *that*, too.

No, the challenge here, the *call to duty* I mean to sound in these pages, is to rediscover our best selves, and the best way I can think for us to do that is to follow these ten guiding principles. I've thought about these principles a lot, about the ways meaningful change has been brought about by people, not institutions, and how it is in the way we live our lives that we lift each other up and move each other forward. To my mind, nothing is more important. These ideas have been a part of my speeches since I first ran for Congress, and they were at the heart of my two campaigns for president, and I return to them here because I truly believe it's on each of us to do our part to set America right.

Those ten principles:

1) *Start a Movement*

   Let's accept that true power flows up—and then, let's do what we can to harness that power. From the women's suffrage movement, to the civil rights movement…from Vietnam to environmental awareness and gun control…we'll take a look at some of the groundswell, grassroots initiatives that have helped shape our political and social landscapes and move our country forward.

2) *Be the Change Where You Live*

   I'll encourage you to set your sights close to home, and to recognize that each of us must do what we can within reach, to make a real difference in our neighborhoods, in the world at hand and the world around.

3) *Be Prepared to Walk a Lonely Road*

   Leadership sometimes means being out in front on an issue or a mission, so let's accept that we might need to stand apart from the crowd before we can find a way to convince others to stand alongside. Know that when you are out in front you will face criticism—but know, too, that in answering your critics with honesty, clarity, and empathy, you will bring others around to your way of thinking.

4) *Slow Down*
Our lives are so frantic we often fail to see what's right in front of us, so here I'll emphasize the importance of taking the time to stop, look, and breathe as we go about our days, highlighting the great rewards to be found in deliberation, consideration, and contemplation.

5) *Bounce Back*
When we suffer a setback, we need to be able to dust ourselves off and put ourselves back in the mix, because it is when we let ourselves be cast as victims that we begin to lose our way, so let's find a way to tap the wellspring of resilience, perseverance, and grit that resides in each of us.

6) *Love Thy Neighbor*
A call to lift each other up, not tear each other down; to heal each other's wounds, not open new ones; to move each other forward, not hold each other back.

7) *Get Out of Your Silo*

To paraphrase the great Dorothy Parker, the cure for boredom is curiosity. Happily, there is no cure for curiosity, and if we're out to survive and thrive as a society we must be vigilant in our pursuit of truth, new information, and challenging ideas. That means getting out of our own silos and reading widely, hungrily, and even indiscriminately. That means taking in other points of view and keeping open to revisiting our own. That means taking the time to study an issue before weighing in on it in a public way. And, just as we must make an effort to keep our world from spinning out of control, we must make the time to listen to our family, our friends, our neighbors, and to carefully consider opinions other than our own.

8) *Put Yourself In Someone Else's Shoes*

Sometimes we need to change our perspective in order to see an issue or a circumstance as it truly appears. The best way to understand someone else's struggle is to imagine what it would be like to be in the same situation, so here I'm out to encourage readers to tap the great wellspring of empathy that surely resides in us all.

9) *Spend Time Examining Your Eternal Destiny*

Life doesn't last forever—and no matter where we stand on the issue of faith, we ought to be thinking about the footprints we're leaving here on this earth and the life that awaits us in the great beyond.

10) *Know That You Are Made Special*

Perhaps the most important bit of guidance I'll offer in these pages—a shout-out to readers that we are all made special. There is only one you. There will never be another quite like you. Know this, embrace this, and live every day in such a way that your individuality shines through.

So there you have it: ten little ways we can bring about big change. Taken together, they offer a roadmap for each of us to follow as we look to live a life bigger than ourselves; taken one by one, they can help to lift us from a place of outrage or complacency or helplessness and move us ever closer to our shared American ideal.

Let's take a look at them, shall we?

1

Start a Movement

There is one thing you have got to learn about our movement. Three people are better than no people.

—Fannie Lou Hamer

Movements matter—absolutely, they do. And get this: each of us has the power to get one started—absolutely, we do.

A lot of us, we pull out our hair and worry about the state of the union, the state of the world. We vent on social media, put lawn signs in our front yard in support of our favorite candidate or issue. We grouse to our friends and family. And then, when something really gets us going, we wonder why *someone* isn't doing *something* about it.

Well, let me put the question back on you: Why aren't *you* doing something about it? Posting stuff on Twitter or Instagram isn't enough. If that's your thing—great, at least you're doing something, but don't let yourself think you're done. Social media is really just a place to start—the modern-day equivalent of a handmade sign at a protest march. It might catch someone's attention, and maybe even provide some kind of spark for a great group of someones, but it won't get you anywhere on its own. Bending someone's ear at a party is another good way to start winning someone over to your way of thinking—but here again, you'll need to do more. So where does that leave us? Maybe all you can do is rally a couple friends to stand with you in the village square to raise your voices in protest or support of an issue, but stand there long enough and another few folks will wander by and ask what you're up to. If your concern has some merit to it, maybe they'll agree with what you have to say and add another few voices to your chorus. Maybe somebody with a camera will happen by, and your small protest will end up on local television, and then a whole bunch of people will see and hear what you're up to and your numbers will grow even more.

Certainly, when we talk about movements on a grand scale, we talk about the civil rights movement. We talk about the protests that fomented on college campuses against the war in Vietnam. We talk about

women's suffrage, and growing environmental awareness. None of these movements succeeded in changing the world in an instant, but all of them succeeded
eventually. Historically, movements happen when people join together for a common cause, when they're
seeking justice or hope or opportunity. They happen when people are passionate about something—or
maybe when folks are feeling up against it, like time is
running out on them and they'd better get up and do
something about whatever it is that's troubling them
or keeping them down. It could be over something as
simple as people wanting to improve their daily lives—
like getting the park commissioner to keep the lights
on at the local ball field so your kids have a place to
play on Friday nights.

For the purposes of this discussion, I want to keep
the focus on the movements we might jump-start in
our own communities, understanding full well that
you can't always count on hitting just the right note,
at just the right time, so that people respond to your
appeal in just the right way. Those who believe other-
wise remind me of the time I sat in a planning meeting with a group trying to get some traction on a new
idea. Someone suggested that we produce a viral video
in support of this new idea—but, alas, viral videos

don't just up and happen. You can't snap your fingers and start trending on social media. To be clear, you can't always trust polling or market research to tell you how people are going to respond to your genuine call to action. And you certainly can't *engineer* genuine. You can only *be* genuine. And, people can only respond in kind.

Before you start telling me you couldn't possibly win a group of people over to your way of thinking in sufficient numbers to get a movement going or to make any kind of difference, I want to introduce you to a girl named Greta Thunberg. Perhaps you've heard of her. She's the young climate change activist from Sweden who was nominated for a Nobel Peace Prize for her work organizing the world's first school strike for climate change. Her story is incredible because there's no magic to it. It's straightforward. It's genuine. And, it's connected to the "be the change where you live" theme that will continue this conversation in the next chapter. Like those mourners in Toronto, Greta Thunberg basically showed up. Like little Flo in Chicago, she got the folks in her community to buy in to her message.

But here's the thing: Greta Thunberg didn't set out to go viral. She didn't intend to start a global movement. She only wanted to be heard. By her own admission, she was uncomfortable talking in front of large groups of people. She was diagnosed with Asperger's syndrome when she was a little girl, but she didn't let that stop her from doing well in school— or from learning about the environment, which had become an issue of great concern to her. And yet the more she studied our developing climate crisis, the more she wanted to lift her voice on behalf of her generation. So she made a couple signs and started holding them up outside the Swedish parliament. In particular, she was worried about a series of devastating heat waves and wildfires in Sweden and believed it was her responsibility to demand that the government follow the guidelines of the Paris climate agreement and reduce carbon emissions.

Keep in mind, she was only fifteen years old.

After a while, people started to notice, and a while after *that* Greta put it out there that she would not attend school until the next general election—and it was at this point that the media started paying attention. The sight of this Swedish schoolgirl standing her ground in this small, simple way seemed to stir something in a whole lot of people, who perhaps heard in Greta's words a plaintive cry on behalf of the world's children.

When the election came and went, and Greta's "demands" had still not been met, she continued her boycott on Fridays—realizing, I guess, that school was kind of important and that she couldn't justify all that time away from the classroom if she expected to be taken seriously on this.

Over time, students all over the world were encouraged to take up Greta's fight, and a global movement was born. Best I can tell, she no longer seems to mind being on a public stage. She addressed the United Nations Climate Conference in Katowice, Poland, the World Economic Forum in Davos, and an influential TED Talks audience in Stockholm— pretty amazing stuff for someone so young. But it's what she does when she has your full and undivided attention that rates a mention here. What she does is speak honestly and passionately about an issue of pressing concern to her, and to young people around the world. That's the key, really, when you're out to inspire. Your mission needs to come from a genuine place, and you need to be able to put it out there in such a way that it connects with people and echoes some of their own concerns.

Then, at last, you'll get a hearing.

It was Greta who spearheaded the global climate strike by hundreds of thousands of schoolchildren, hoping to make their voices heard (and their absences felt) on the issue of climate change—an especially powerful protest because, really, it's the world's children who will be most impacted by our systemic failure to address our climate crisis in a meaningful way.

And it was Greta who inspired hundreds of young climate warriors all over the world, risking their education and their standing at school to lead their own local strikes for climate change action.

How did someone so young galvanize a generation to stand with her on this issue? She raised her voice, and opened her heart, and people were inspired to fall in alongside.

In interviews, Greta has talked about how she in turn was inspired by the students from Marjory Stoneman Douglas High School in Parkland, Florida, who stood together in grief and anger to protest our gun control laws following the dreadful shooting at their school in February 2018 that resulted in the deaths of seventeen students and staff members. In the wake of the shooting, a number of Parkland students emerged from the ashes of that tragedy to lead a nationwide call for more sensible gun control laws. As readers will surely remember, there were marches and rallies across the country—around the world, even—beneath the #NeverAgain social media hashtag. These brave teenagers had only to lift their voices while the world was listening and, over time, their shared passion helped to change our national conversation on this issue.

These young men and women from Parkland had survived an unthinkable tragedy, a horrific slaughter, and out of that they opened their hearts…and people listened. Less than a month after the shooting, Florida lawmakers passed a gun control and school safety bill that raised the minimum age to purchase firearms from eighteen to twenty-one, banned the sale of machine-gun-type weapons known as bump stocks, imposed a three-day waiting period on all gun purchases, and provided increased funding for school counselors and school police officers. All across the country, other state legislators started looking seriously at their own gun laws in response to the overwhelming public outcry on this issue.

There's no way for me to overstate the real and profound impact these students made in the name of sensible gun laws. Prior to the Parkland shooting, Florida legislators had never shown any interest in gun control laws, just as Florida residents had never really lobbied for them in quite this way, but these students demanded them. Really, it was an extraordinary thing to see, an awesome achievement, and what was especially impressive was the way these students soldiered on once they started getting attacked on social media and threatened in their community. It was appalling to see—a tragedy on top of a tragedy!—the way these kids became targets simply for standing up for what they believed was the right thing to do, but they kept at it, undaunted. They made it clear to Florida lawmakers that this was what their constituents wanted. They were unified, and spoke with a powerful voice, and knew how to use social media to advantage.

This last was key, and even though I wrote earlier that posts on Twitter and Instagram and Facebook aren't enough to move the needle on their own, social media can complement our efforts on the ground. In particular, those social media hashtags can be galvanizing tools, wouldn't you agree? They're not a replacement for real and tangible action, but they can offer a mighty reinforcement to a message or a movement that is gathering support. Here the message at the heart of the movement was #NeverAgain. In Greta's case, it was #FridaysForFuture. These little signatures are the modern-day equivalent of the chants we used to hear at marches and protest rallies: "Hell no, we won't go!"…"We shall overcome!"…and on and on.

They are rallying cries for change.

Crowds matter, too—in fact, that's how most movements are measured at the outset. That said, a *groundswell of support* is a relative thing, so as you get going, be sure to keep your expectations consistent with the size of your campaign. In other words, don't be discouraged if you're only able to organize a dozen or so supporters on a local issue, because that might be just the number you need to get the attention of a local official. But those same dozen supporters won't amount to a whole lot on a national issue, so try to be realistic as you move forward. Be prepared to change your strategy, or to reach out to like-minded souls in other communities who might be inclined to take up your cause, because you need to find a way to make sure your voices are heard if you want to bring about meaningful change. As someone who's held public office, let me assure you that those unified voices matter. Consistent calls matter. Coordinated efforts matter. Whether we like it or not, the squeaky wheel always seems to get the grease, and no politician wants to stand on the wrong side of fervent, determined, and thoughtful opposition on an issue.

One of the great things about movements is that you don't have to be the person who starts the movement to help advance the conversation. Change the world in whatever way you can, using whatever skill set you can bring to the task, but do your part. Some people are going to play a complicated piece on the violin, and some people are going to ding the bell, but in an orchestra every instrument matters. They all fit together to make the music that moves us…so go ahead and move us, and as you do, know that there is strength in numbers.

Another great thing about movements is that they are a team effort. You don't have to go it alone. In fact, you can't. A movement without a base of support probably won't be effective, so reach out for help along the way. We have this wonderful concept in our society known as the handoff. You push a project or a notion or a really big issue as far as you can, and then you hand it off to someone who can carry it the rest of the way. It's like running a relay race. You go hard until you run out of steam and pass the baton to the next person. A lot of times, for a lot of reasons, we're not able to finish the race, but that doesn't mean we shouldn't start.

It takes time to effect real change. And a certain amount of knowing how to navigate the system. But know this as well: for the most part, governments don't bring about change on a societal level. No, *real* change, *fundamental* change almost always happens in a bottom-up sort of way. The people tell us what they want to see happen, and if they're mindful about it… and sincere…and persuasive and persistent in their arguments…well, they're almost always going to be able to get their elected officials on board to help them realize their shared vision. Our elected officials are not about to show up at a town hall and start arguing against a movement based on justice and fairness. To do so would be to jeopardize their careers as elected officials—because, let's face it, the politicians work for us. *We* don't work for *them*. And so when we're clear in what we want, when we're on the right side of an issue and able to communicate our position forcefully, we'll likely prevail.

I'll give you a great example of the way change can happen in a bottom-up way—and in this particular case it took almost no time at all. As I write this, a lot of folks are still reeling from the Trump administration's plan to cut funding for the Special Olympics. Recall, when the Trump budget was presented in March 2019, it contained an overall reduction in the Department of Education budget of about $7.1 billion—or, 10 percent. Included in the budget were proposed cuts of $18 million for the Special Olympics, representing a little more than 12 percent of the organization's overall budget.

(For context, note that the bulk of the Special Olympics program is funded through private donations, but these federal monies are traditionally earmarked for school-based initiatives for children with disabilities.)

The response to these proposed cuts was overwhelmingly negative. The American people cried foul. The cuts were aimed at an iconic social program that had become a part of the fabric of our culture—it's very name synonymous with the call to stand up for children with special needs and their families. And so the people let it be known in no uncertain terms that this population was a priority, and that these proposed cuts would not stand. They were unkind, unjust, and it had nothing to do with political party affiliation. Democrats and Republicans alike lined up in support of the Special Olympics, demanding that the cuts be restored. The backlash was swift, and heated, and the remonstrations continued across social media and in traditional media outlets. The indignation was such that it outlasted the typical twenty-four-hour news cycle, and it became quickly apparent that this one simple line-item would be an ongoing nightmare for the president and his subordinates.

And so, just a couple days after the proposed budget was first circulated, President Trump himself announced in an impromptu gaggle on the White House lawn that he had just told his "people" to restore the cuts. Why? Because *our* "people" had spoken in such a loud, forceful way that the White House had no choice but to listen—and with the stroke of a pen, essentially, a miscalculation made from on high was corrected.

Granted, it's unusual to see such an abrupt about-face in government policy at the federal level, but the power of our collective voices can be an immutable force for change. It's up to us to use that force for good. When you are in the right, when the public is on your side, change can happen in the space of a single news cycle.

Sometimes, movements take on organic shape in ways that can be inspiring, and here I want to turn your attention to an outpouring of support on behalf of a Puerto Rican icon. This particular movement struck a particular chord with me because as a kid from the outskirts of Pittsburgh, my favorite baseball player was Roberto Clemente. The few times I went to Forbes Field to see a ball game in person, he was the first player I looked for down on the field during the pregame warm-ups. I'd fix on him in that pristine Pirates jersey with his number on the back—#21—and it was that number that stood at the heart of this movement. Clemente was the closest thing I had to a boyhood hero, and when he died in a plane crash while on a relief mission to Nicaragua in 1972, it was one of the only times I saw my mother cry. We were all shaken by Clemente's death, and now, all these years later, I am shaken again by the way today's Puerto Rican–born players have chosen to honor his memory.

The story came to my attention earlier this year on Jackie Robinson Day—April 15—the day Major League Baseball has chosen to honor the man who broke the game's color barrier on that date in 1947. Since 2004, as some readers might know, all players, coaches, managers, and even the umpires wear Jackie Robinson's uniform number on their jerseys—#42— to commemorate his life and legacy. (By the way, that number was retired across all of baseball in 1997.) However, a push to honor Roberto Clemente in a similar way has been repeatedly rebuffed, with Major League Baseball commissioner Rob Manfred declaring that different players deserve to be honored in different ways. To be sure—and, to be fair—each year the league gives out the prestigious Roberto Clemente Award to the player who best embodies Clemente's spirit of sportsmanship and service, and many consider it one of baseball's highest honors, so I'm not suggesting here that the game has turned its back on the Pirate Hall of Famer.

And yet Puerto Rican players have *effectively* retired Clemente's number by refusing to wear it. For some, it's a way of honoring their hero that goes all the way back to their childhoods. For example, Eddie Rosario, a left fielder for the Minnesota Twins, told the *New York Times* about the time he was offered a #21 jersey in one of his Puerto Rican youth leagues.

"I'm not Roberto Clemente," he'd told his manager at the time. "I can't wear that."

A lot of players feel the same way. According to the *Times*, only sixteen Puerto Rican–born players have worn that number in a major league game since Clemente's death in 1972, out of a possible 235—and not a single player has worn the number in the past five years. What started as an informal show of respect has become a movement to celebrate a man who was known as much for his prowess on the field as for the way he stood as a champion to all Latino players and a force in the fight against segregation—and I share the story here for the way it reminds us that we don't always need the permission or approval of our elected officials or our governing bodies to bring about change.

Sometimes, all it takes is doing what you know to be righteous and good and true—and, for the record, it certainly helps if you're standing with a groundswell of support.

Now, *starting* a movement is key, but let's not discount the importance of *joining* a movement. After all, if nobody throws in with you on an issue then all you've really got is a false start—so along with true leadership comes something I call *followship*, which refers to the qualities we expect to find in those falling into step behind the leaders in their midst.

And speaking of followship, let's not forget how important it is to have people around us to offer a kind of reality check. Leaders need followers to let them know if their concerns are real, if their strategies are sound, if the changes they're seeking are even possible…basically, a kind of sounding board to determine the efficacy of an idea. Understand, I'm not talking about assembling a kind of "amen chorus" to fall in blindly behind us and echo our points of view. No, what's needed is a collection of objective, reasonable people who perhaps share our concerns and are uniquely positioned to weigh in on whether or not we're moving in the right direction.

When I ran for president last time, I put together a kind of punch list of qualities we look for in our leaders *and* in our followers—because, of course, the two go hand in hand. Take a look and see if you can recognize some of these traits in yourself, as you seek to make a difference and make *your* movement matter:

1) *Leaders need to have a vision*: without a clear call to action that offers hope for the future, you'll never line up the support you'll need to get out of the gate...

2) *Followers must let it be known that they share in that vision*: you'll need to know in the early going that people are responding to that call...

3) *Leaders need to develop a team*: there ought to be some level of consensus building, and delegat-

ing of authority, as you set off in pursuit of your shared goal…you might start out as a kind of lone wolf, but you can't go it alone indefinitely…

4) *Followers must take on subordinate roles in this dynamic until they're comfortable stepping out in front and taking on more of a leadership role*: there must emerge a group of supporters who assent to your direction and leadership, and look to enhance that direction and leadership as your cause gains momentum…

5) *Leaders need to keep reinforcing their vision*: it's not enough to simply state your ideas or your objectives and then put the whole thing on autopilot… no, you must tend and nurture your mission, perhaps even allowing for a course-correction or two along the way…

6) *Followers must be willing to disrupt the status quo*: if it happens that you start to lean the wrong way, or reach for a shortcut that somehow undermines your stated mission, it's helpful to have someone in the ranks who will keep you honest and help

you refocus… What you're looking for here is *constructive* criticism, not *destructive* criticism…

And so I put the question back to you, just as I did at the start of this chapter, this time with a couple of follow-ups: What are you doing to make your voice heard on the issues that matter to you?

What can you do better?

Are you ready to start a whole new conversation?

2

Be the Change Where You Live

If you have only one smile in you,
give it to the people you love.

—Maya Angelou

If the idea of starting a national movement feels a little too big or just out of reach, let's turn our attention close to home. That's where we can have the biggest impact on the world in which we live, because it's a world within reach.

One of the best illustrations of this is a giant of a man I once knew named Albert Lexie. I've written about Albert before, and I've talked about him on the campaign trail and throughout my career. Truth is, I can't say enough about Albert, so I hope you'll forgive me if you've heard his story already, but he's been on my mind since his sad passing in October 2018. I see his face every time I think about what it means to make a difference, and I imagine that when Albert died, the late obituary writer Jim Nicholson could have written one of his most glowing tributes in his memory.

As "nobodies" go, Albert Lexie was certainly somebody—and it was an honor to get to know him.

Let me tell you about Albert. He never finished high school, but his impact on his community was as significant as any scholar, as any emergency room nurse or real estate developer. Albert was a shoeshine man who worked a couple days each week for most of his adult life at Children's Hospital in Pittsburgh, where he lived. He carried the tools of his trade in a shoeshine box he'd built himself in shop class when he was in eighth grade—the last year he attended school.

How Albert came to Children's Hospital is worth remembering. One night, after he'd been shining shoes for almost thirty years, he saw a Children's Hospital telethon on KDKA-TV in Pittsburgh and was struck by the story of a young girl who was featured on the air. Something about this little girl touched Albert's heart in a life-changing way, so he went to his bank the next morning and withdrew every dollar he had, about eight hundred dollars, and walked with the cash to the hospital to make a donation.

At first, he couldn't even find anyone to accept the donation, but he was finally directed to the right department, and when hospital administrators learned of this particular kindness they reached back to Albert and offered him a spot in the lobby for his shoeshine business. Their thought was to return a kindness with a kindness—but that's a whole other story.

One of the things I loved about Albert was that he marched to his own beat. He didn't think he could fit the hospital into his busy schedule, didn't see that he'd be any better off shining shoes beneath the fluorescent lights of the hospital lobby than he'd be outside on one of his usual corners in the dead of winter, so his first thought was to stiff-arm the offer. He had his regular customers at his regular haunts all over the city, and he enjoyed his routines, but he eventually agreed to give the hospital two days a week of his time. This was no small consideration on Albert's part, because the hospital was an hour-plus bus ride from his home, and he'd have to lug his thirty-pound shoeshine box the whole way, filled with every style of brush and polish for every style of shoe leather. Long story short: he ended up making that round-trip every Tuesday and Thursday for the rest of his working life, and during that time he became such a fixture at the hospital that nobody blinked when they saw all these doctors and nurses and family members of patients walking around in their socks because they'd left their shoes with Albert for a shine.

After that first $800, Albert wasn't done giving. In the beginning, he charged three dollars for a shine, and he'd put that money in one pocket so he could cover his rent, his groceries, his electric bill, and his bus fare. Whatever he earned in tips, he'd put it in another pocket, and he'd take that set-aside money and return it right back to the hospital, to add to his original donation. As he raised his rates, he stuck to the same business model—one pocket for him, and one pocket for the kids. Over the years, it was determined that he'd given over $202,000 to the Children's Hospital's Free Care Fund—an astonishing total, when you stop to think that it all came from tips and from the goodness of this one man's heart.

By the time of his death, Albert had been honored by a bunch of news and philanthropic organizations, and in 2006 he was inducted into the Hall of Fame for Caring Americans by the Caring Institute, but he didn't do what he did for recognition. He did it to make a difference—and boy, did he make a difference. And it was a difference he could see, because he made it a special point to stop in and visit some of the kids in the hospital every week.

That's the great and lasting benefit of doing good works in your community—you get to have a hand in those good works going forward. You get to see the benefits every day. And the folks on the receiving end of your generosity get to see you as well, so they're more inclined to pay your kindness forward, if they're ever in a position to do so.

What we can learn from a man like Albert Lexie is the enormous power of doing what you can, where you can. Probably, before he just happened on that telethon on television, he didn't know the first thing about Children's Hospital or its mission. Probably, he'd never given a thought to how families with chronically ill or terminally ill children might pay their bills—or how they might accommodate a long hospital stay. But after seeing these kids and learning about the challenges they faced, he made it a priority to do what he could to help them out. And the thing with Albert was he didn't just donate his tip money and call it a day. He spent time in the unit, got to know the children, the families, the doctors, the nurses. He brought a little bit of light and joy to these folks working in the toughest of circumstances, and it all flowed from the magic of that shoeshine box.

He gave of himself—and he did it in such a way that he could be a part of the good he was looking to put back out into his little corner of Pittsburgh.

There are champions like Albert Lexie in *every* community—all over the world, in fact. When I traveled with my wife, Karen, to Rwanda, just to offer one compelling example, we sat with a woman who'd been raped, macheted, beaten, and left for dead by the side of a river, and yet out of that experience this woman had somehow found the strength and grace to lead a group of women, who had been similarly victimized, to come together seeking forgiveness for those who'd committed these atrocities. It was the summer of 2008, and we were there on behalf of the ONE Campaign, a nonpartisan advocacy group co-founded by Bono of the Irish rock band U2 to fight poverty and preventable disease all over the world, particularly in Africa. Our traveling party for this trip included Cindy McCain, wife of my great friend Senator John McCain, who of course was back in the States running for president that summer; former Senate Majority Leader Bill Frist; former Arkansas governor Mike Huckabee; political consultant John

Podesta, the former White House chief of staff under Bill Clinton; and a handful of innovators and executives from Google. It really was an eye-opening trip, and Karen and I were especially struck by this one encounter with this proud, grace-filled woman at a luncheon that had been arranged for us at Hôtel des Milles Collines, which we recognized as the setting for the movie *Hotel Rwanda*.

As we sat down to lunch, Karen's dining companion had yet to arrive, so she took her place next to an empty seat. I sat on the other side of that empty seat, next to this Rwandan woman, and she told me of her struggle during the Rwandan Civil War, and the longstanding tensions between the Hutu and Tutsi tribes. Early on in our conversation, the seat between Karen and I was finally filled—by a young man named Patrick. To Karen's great shock, Patrick was a stone-cold killer, who in the wake of the Rwandan genocide and the great reconciliation led by President Paul Kagame had been made to apologize for his crimes and was now living among the very people who had once been his sworn enemies, including the families of some of his victims. It really was a remarkable turn of events, but that's how things were in Rwanda at the time of our visit. There was no room in the nation's prison system to incarcerate the war criminals, so those facing judgment were often asked to make amends in their own communities, and as Karen spoke with Patrick, she could hear the genuine pain and remorse in his voice. She told me later that she was inspired at the way these sworn enemies had been encouraged to come together to live a life of purpose and meaning in a unified Rwanda.

Can you imagine that? Somehow through their unknowable pain and anguish, these women, led in part by my luncheon companion, recognized that the only way for Rwanda to heal, the only way to move forward and build an environment where their children could grow up free from the torment that had stamped their own lives, was to find it in their hearts to try to build a bridge between a hateful, hurtful past and a hopeful future. And, on the other side of that great divide, there were people like Patrick, grateful for the chance to step from the darkness of their murderous pasts and live in the light with their neighbors.

As we pulled away from the hotel following the luncheon, we noticed Patrick standing with this woman and talking amiably, enjoying each other's company in a way I'm sure neither could have imagined just a few years earlier.

Forgiveness can be a powerful tool, and when it finds you close to home this is especially so. That's how I felt the first time I met Rachel Muha—my goodness, Rachel's story is heartbreaking, but underneath the heartbreak it's also uplifting. Rachel had a son named Brian, who was a student at Franciscan University in Steubenville, Ohio. Brian and a friend of his, Aaron Land, were kidnapped not far from campus and driven to the woods in Pennsylvania, where they were brutally murdered. It was just awful. It took the police a full week to find the bodies of those young men, and when they did Rachel was devastated. *Flattened*, really. But she knew, even in those terrible moments when the details of her son's final hours were made clear to her, that she had to find a way to forgive the two young men charged with his murder. What got her thinking in this way more than anything else was the anger and hatred she saw from her nephews over what had happened to her son. These young men were so outraged and devastated by their cousin's murder that they vowed some type of vengeance, but Rachel knew anger and hatred were not the answer. She knew it was on her to help to turn the page for her family, and for her community, and by some miracle of faith and charity, she did—and out of that the two gang members who killed her son inspired her to start a foundation to help "at risk" kids, and steer them down a positive path.

The upshot? Rachel now runs an after-school and summer program on the west side of Columbus, offering spiritual guidance, programming, and support services for inner-city youth, hoping to create an environment where troubled kids might flourish. Since she opened her doors in 2005, Rachel's Run the Race Center has served over five hundred students and families, becoming a kind of second home for those who are unable to find the guidance and support they need in their first home—and all of this came about on the back of this unthinkable personal nightmare.

"The minute you are willing to forgive, it changes everything," she told a local reporter, who came by to do a story on Rachel's program.

Yes, it does.

I see people like Albert Lexie and Rachel Muha on the same continuum as the folks I introduced you to in the opening pages of this book. Like that hostess at the Chuck E. Cheese's in Queens and the rabbi from Toronto, they recognized a hole in their community and moved to fill it. Like little Flo from Chicago, they took it on themselves to make a difference in what ways they could, solving big picture–type problems with small strokes.

The idea, really, is to set out to heal the world in ways we can see and touch, because if we allow ourselves to think that our problems are too big or too complicated to address, we'll never get anywhere. It's not about what we *can't* do—it's about what we *can* do. And what we can do, when we start to peck away at these problems as individuals, is just about anything. All it takes is doing. And caring. And, most of all, keeping open to those moments that find us each day where a little bit of help or comfort or counsel might be needed and it turns out we're uniquely positioned to offer it.

So what can you do once you decide you want to be an agent of change in your hometown? How do you even know where to start? It's pretty straightforward, when you break it down, and it comes from keeping open to the world around you. Open your mind, open your eyes, and you'll find what needs doing. You will. And then, once you've been stirred by a cause or an issue or a need, and processed all the different ways you might be able to help, you've got to get out of your chair and have at it. I tell people it's like going to the local pool once you've decided you want to take up swimming. You can talk about it all you want. You can stand on the pool deck and dip your toes in the water. But at some point you've got to jump in and start swimming.

What are your special skills? Are you a good communicator? A good motivator? A good organizer? Have people told you that you're a good listener, or that you're blessed with the gift of compassion? Or maybe it's been pointed out to you that you're good with your hands, or creative in a way that could help to get people excited about an issue. Whatever the problem, whatever the need, take some time to analyze the situation and see how you might fit yourself into the solution. You might recognize a way to unleash a special passion that's been burning within you going back as far as you can remember, or you might discover a way to bridge an impasse between two people or two groups of people. The idea is to be on the lookout for opportunities that come your way. You don't have to cure polio, or negotiate peace in the Middle East, or rescue someone from the top of Mount Everest. But you do have to take the time to see what's going on, and to see if there might be some way for you to make things better.

When you travel the country the way I do, when

you visit with people in their local churches and schools and in their very own homes, you get to see a side of America that doesn't always shine through. You see people at their very best. You see people as they are. When you run for president, you see these things in a kind of turbocharged way, and I've come to appreciate that the view we take in at ground level is far more intimate, far more *real*, than the one that finds us at thirty thousand feet. In other words, the big picture of how we live and work is only made clear in the small snapshots that find us along the way, the collection of moments and memories we assemble as we move about our days. Change doesn't happen all at once, on a global scale. It finds us in an incremental way—one good turn at a time, one day at a time—until after a while we look up and see that the kindness or generosity we've put out into the world has spread.

Remember the message at the heart of this book: *nothing good is lost*. Every small good thing accrues to the greater good. It does.

Sometimes it happens that change comes about with a push from those in need—and I've got a story to illustrate this learned truth, as well. Toward the end of my second term as governor, I was visited by a dozen or so teenage girls from various broken homes in Pike County,

in Appalachian Ohio. The visit was set up through the
Speaker of the House, whose district happened to cover
this rural part of the state, and spearheaded by a local
police officer, Captain Dennis Crabtree, and the girls'
school guidance counselor, Courtney Gullion-Gillott,
who saw that these girls were struggling because their
parents were failing them, and because there was no
system in place to help set things right.

Let me tell you, when these girls came to see me
in the cabinet room at the Statehouse, I was over-
whelmed by their stories. Their home lives were a
mess. Their parents were in and out of jail, in and
out of rehab programs. They talked about how there
was never any food in the house, no adult supervi-
sion, sometimes no utilities because their parents could
never manage to pay the bills…the kind of chaos that
finds you when you live in a household with virtually
no parental guidance. Some of the girls had stopped
going to school altogether—not because they were
bad kids, but because they were in a bad way. The
girls were in a particularly tough spot because many
of them were too old for foster care and too young to
emancipate themselves, and quite a few of them felt
responsible for helping to care for their younger sib-
lings. They'd gotten together and decided that simply

by meeting with the governor and the Speaker of the House they could somehow be returned to the lives they once had or believed they should have.

I remember thinking it was a remarkable thing that these girls had the wherewithal to connect with my team on something like this—and, just being honest, my first thought was to free up some money in the budget to see if we could do a better job of funding our social service programs in Appalachian Ohio in ways that might prove helpful. But then as I sat with my team I was made to realize that this was not the type of problem that could be solved with a check. Indeed, the monies we were already spending on social service programs like SNAP—our Supplemental Nutritional Assistance Program—were being intercepted by some of these parents and used to feed their drug addictions. Parents were skipping out on treatment programs before they were completed, and generally scamming the system at every turn, leaving their children in a tailspin of domestic violence, poverty, and neglect.

Sure, we could have been doing a better job to make sure state funds weren't being misused in this way, but that would have only scratched the surface of the problem. The only way to heal this particular community was to find a way to help the community heal itself, so we set about looking for ways to address the problem in a more organic way. What these girls needed, we determined, was a break. They needed a place to go to escape the chaos of their home lives because they were so completely stressed out. There was no room in their days for school, or for developing any interests outside of school.

It was all they could do to just survive—to make it from one day to the next.

By some great miracle of timing and proximity we were able to identify a local YMCA director named Kim Conley who was willing to partner with us on a safe space initiative that would provide these girls with a respite. At the Y, with the guidance of Kim Conley, who had been a former youth coach, they'd have a safe space, somewhere to go outside of school where they could escape some of the stresses of their days, maybe participate in a program or use the gym or get some extra help with their homework.

Out of that alliance, other community leaders were inspired to help out, as well. Walmart and Lowe's donated some money to fund after-school programs and provide much-needed items, while Pfizer made a major donation to our Foundation for Appalachian

Ohio initiative, which we were able to direct to this program. Other local business owners and leaders weighed in. Ohio University even offered a scholarship to one of the girls who was an especially talented dancer.

Really, the outpouring of community support that came out of our initial meeting at the Statehouse was staggering, and when I traveled to Pike County about three months later to see firsthand how these girls were faring, I was struck yet again by the full force of what's possible when meaningful change happens in a bottom-up sort of way.

At one point, I stopped to talk to one of the girls in the program and asked her how her life had changed, now that she had a place to go and people she could talk to about what was going on at home.

She said, "Well, I don't think so much about killing myself all the time now."

Can you imagine? I was floored by this girl's honesty, and at the same time lifted by the hope we'd somehow been able to tap, where there had once been only hopelessness. I had tears in my eyes as I moved on to talk to the other girls in the group, who told me their stories, and as I listened I marveled at the ways these community leaders had been able to galvanize

Pike County's business, education, and faith communities and knit a kind of safety net for these young women, who were now looking ahead to their bright futures despite their home lives.

As a footnote, I'm even happier to report that the program we put in place here was being replicated in a handful of other counties by the time I left office. Just as this Pike County community was able to rally together, other leaders emerged who reached out to us to help them deal with rural poverty issues in their areas, and with this template in place we were able to jumpstart initiatives all across the state. Even if we had the money in our budget to do anything more than subsidize these efforts, money alone would not have been enough. We needed to help these folks identify solutions inside the framework of their communities, to find local leaders to help take on some of these issues and in so doing find a way to help themselves.

The great takeaway from this Pike County initiative, for me, was the compelling reminder that those in a position to make a difference don't always know what they can do to help—or even that their help might be needed. When you look to lead, there needs to be someone looking to be led—meaning, you need at least one follower. Everybody's a leader to somebody. We don't have to stand on a great stage or hold a big job in order to make an impact. My wife, for example, is a leader to our daughters. Oh, she's so much more than that: as Ohio's first lady, she helped to lead the fight against human trafficking, and now that I'm out of office she continues to work in support of underprivileged, underserved, and undervalued women in our community. But every day she lights a path our girls might follow, and she's always available to talk them through a bad patch or difficulty—and to stand as a shining example. My daughters, in turn, are able to take on the same role for each other, and for some of their friends, so it's the kind of thing that turns in on itself and keeps going.

How do we make a difference in the lives of the people around us? Well, I believe it starts with paying good and close attention. But attention alone doesn't cut it if it's not accompanied by *intention*. Yes, we need to be plugged in to our family and friends in ways that signal to us when our help might be needed…and then we need to step up and do something about it.

Our communities are our touchstones: we live and breathe in our commitment to each other. And yet we live such fast-paced lives, often in isolation, that it can be tough to know how our neighbors are doing, or what they're up to. Even in our biggest cities, we can sometimes feel alone together—meaning, we're stuck in our own orbit, focused on our own *stuff*, even as we're surrounded by the folks upstairs, downstairs, next door, across the street, and clear across town. Where we should be bound by proximity and all these common points of reference, we are all too often moving to circumstances entirely our own.

Did you know studies show that casual conversation helps to keep us better connected? That's one of the great side benefits of stopping in to check up on your neighbors—one of the reasons my father took the time to stop and make a little bit of small talk here and there as he delivered the mail. He didn't do this *just* for the people on his route; he did it, I'm sure, for himself as well, probably on the learned truth that happiness loves good company, and when you delivered the mail in McKees Rocks, Pennsylvania, there was good company all around.

If you've got an elderly neighbor, or if you live next door to someone who has a little difficulty getting around, why not check in on him or her and see if they need anything the next time you go to the store? Why not shovel the sidewalk in front of their home after it snows? Or grab their newspaper from the curb

and toss it onto their porch when you're out to collect yours on a rainy day? Help fix their mailbox if it
falls off its post, or offer to walk their dog when the
weather's lousy. There's no end to the little things you
can do to brighten someone's day or ease someone's
burden—better yet, enlist your children to help in
this way and maybe get them started on a lifetime of
giving and caring.

These small kindnesses add up, in that incremental way I talked about earlier, and we'll do well to restore a sense of community and connectedness in what
ways we can. There's no looking away from the fact
that our "networks of civic engagement" are not what
they used to be—that's a term used by Harvard University public policy professor Robert D. Putnam, in
his excellent book *Bowling Alone*, which takes a look
at what he suggests is a decline in what he calls our
"social capital," and I offer it here as a kind of opening salvo in these pages to remind us that we are not
in this thing alone.

Our nation is only as strong as our communities,
and our communities are only as strong as the individuals within those communities, so let's make
an extra effort to look at how we might enrich our

neighborhoods before we start worrying over how to fix America.

I have a feeling that if we start taking care of one, the other will follow.

3

Be Prepared to Walk
a Lonely Road

Do what you feel in your heart to be right, for you'll be criticized anyway.

—Eleanor Roosevelt

Something to keep in mind if you're thinking of starting a movement of your own or getting out in front of an issue: you're going to face a lot of criticism along the way, and you might have to go it alone for a good long while.

Even if you're looking to bring about change in your own community in ways that don't involve government or any of your local institutions, you're bound to take some heat, so you should know this going in. And if you're out to make a principled stand that somehow cuts against what others stand for or what others expect of you…well, then you'll get your fair share of slings and arrows as well, even if history might ultimately celebrate the courage of your convictions.

I'm thinking here of the way Sandy Koufax was at first put down by Dodgers fans and sportswriters when he famously refused to pitch Game 1 of the 1965 World Series because it fell on Yom Kippur, the holiest day on the Jewish calendar, only to be embraced and respected by generations of Jews (and others!) who came to see him over time as a powerful role model for sticking to his personal religious beliefs in the face of a very public professional conflict. More than forty years earlier, some readers might recall, the Scottish runner and Christian missionary Eric Liddell was similarly torn when he scratched from the qualifying heats for the 100 meters at the 1924 Summer Olympics in Paris, a race he was favored to win, because they were being held on a Sunday—a story that was later dramatized in the movie *Chariots of Fire*, reminding us of the pressures Liddell faced to set aside his faith and run for his country.

For a more contemporary example, look no further than former Portland Trail Blazers center Enes Kanter, who'd never played in the month of Ramadan during the first seven years of his NBA career. This was significant because Kanter, a practicing Muslim from

Turkey, traditionally commemorates the month that God revealed the Quran to the Prophet Muhammad, requiring him to fast from dawn to sunset. This alone was not so unusual, because over one and a half billion people observe in the same way, but when Kanter's team made the play-offs following the 2018–2019 season, this meant that for the first time he would be called on to keep the faith and somehow maintain his strength and fitness during a grueling postseason schedule.

Think about that for a moment: it's tough enough to go without eating for most of the day without flagging, but this man was somehow able to compete at the very highest level in a brutally demanding sport, helping his team to reach the Western Conference Finals against the Golden State Warriors.

Admirably, Kanter's convictions extend into the political arena, as well. He's been an outspoken critic of Turkish president Tayyip Erdoğan in ways that have threatened Kanter's freedom and his family. As a result, his family back in Turkey has disowned him, and yet he continues to question the actions and policies of the Erdoğan regime, and he regularly reaches out to Republicans and Democrats in Congress to discuss human rights violations in Turkey.

It is, he maintains, the right thing to do—the *only* thing to do—even if it means he must stand alone.

It's never easy to stand alone or rock the boat or upset the status quo. Whatever you're doing that you're *not* supposed to be doing, whatever you're *not* doing that you're supposed to be doing, you should expect to take your hits, no matter how righteous or principled your position. It comes with the territory, but history almost always teaches us that you'll do well to hang in there. You might not change the world on the back of your convictions, but if your cause is just, your intentions sincere, and your actions consistent with your goals, you'll eventually change some hearts and minds and win a bunch of people over to your position—and, even more than that, you'll be able to look back with pride at the way you stuck to what you thought was right.

I'm thinking here of my friend Jim Lynch, my longtime director of communications, who's discovering as he embarks on his own political career that it's not so easy to go it alone. While I was still in office, Jim was encouraged to run for a seat on the city council in Upper Arlington, in Franklin County. He ran because he didn't like some of the things that were going on in his community and thought he was in a position to try to set things right, but once he took office he found that his unwillingness to align with each member of the city council on many issues wasn't always appreciated. Sometimes, he tells me, he's the only vote to go against the majority, but he sticks to his convictions and continues to heed his own call, ignoring the pressures he sometimes faces from party leadership.

That's how it goes when you take the lead—in government, in business, in sports, and in life. Front-runners in all walks of life understand this. Leaders and visionaries understand this. When there are no footsteps for you to follow, no voices to cheer you along and point the way, it can sometimes feel like you're alone in the fight, off in pursuit of a goal only you can see. And it's not just leaders who are made to suffer the judgment of others, or the isolation that often comes with taking the lead on an issue. It can be anyone with the strength of character to call out an injustice—a parent on the sidelines of a Little League game, say, who challenges the abusive behavior of one of the coaches, or an airline employee with the temerity to question the way his colleagues forcibly removed a passenger from an overbooked plane.

When the compass points aren't exactly clear and

there's no map for you to follow, all you can do is all you can do. Here again, I want to stress how important it is to surround yourself with thoughtful, objective supporters who are able to set you straight if you veer off course. I didn't really have a whole lot of people in that role when I started out in politics, save for my close aide and friend Don Thibault. At twenty-five years old, I'd run for the Ohio state senate on a central promise: I would not vote to raise taxes. For the first two years I was in office, we were in the minority, so I was never called on to take another position, but in my third year the Republicans were finally in charge and some of my colleagues thought a tax increase was the only way to close a pretty big budget gap. I believed there was a better way and refused to go back on my promise to voters, but as soon as I made it clear that I would not support a tax increase, I started getting all kinds of pressure. My colleagues were all over me—calling me names, even. *Irresponsible*...that's what they say about you when you refuse to follow the party line. I heard that and thought, *Okay, they think I'm irresponsible, so I'll just go out and prove them wrong.*

How did I do that, exactly? I crafted my own proposal to try and close the budget gap. Don Thibault and I went through every nook and cranny of the entire state budget, looking for expenditures we could trim, programs we could privatize, priorities we could set aside for the next while. Don's support was vital—in fact, I might never have taken up the fight without it. But with the encouragement of my friend and colleague, I was able to press forward. In the beginning, we were getting hammered for our efforts, but something interesting happened over time. I started hearing from some of my Republican colleagues with helpful suggestions. Sometimes, ideas would come to me anonymously, from folks who didn't want it known they were working in support of my idea. One staffer even knocked on my office door late at night, when he thought no one else was around, and he sat with me and pored over the budget suggesting places I could look for cuts.

Out of that experience, I learned more about the operation of the state of Ohio than I would have learned in another decade in office—and I was true to my word, offering a budget proposal that didn't call for a tax increase. That was the good news. The bad news was that my budget didn't pass, but it paved the way for me to think along these lines in the future, and when I got to Congress two years later and

eventually fought my way onto the budget commit-
tee I knew the effort would help me to better understand the entire operations of our federal government.
As Yogi Berra used to say, it was like déjà vu all over
again, and the next time I presented my own budget
in defiance of my own party I at least had a little experience to fall back on.

Now, I don't mean to suggest here that I was blazing
any kind of new trail, or taking a Koufax-like stand—
but, once again, there was nobody outside of my own
office lining up in support of my idea. If you go back
and read some of the news accounts from that time,
you'll see notes and comments from some of my colleagues on the Hill, wondering what had gotten into
me. Even my own hometown newspapers couldn't
figure out what to make of me. To them, it was like
I was beating my head against the wall. You have to
realize, the federal budget hadn't been balanced since
1969, but I thought we should do something about
that—for the simple reason that it was the right thing
to do. President Bush had just proposed his first budget and I thought it was pretty terrible. The Democrats countered with a proposal that I thought was
even worse. And yet on each side of the aisle there
was the sense that we had only this binary choice—

that we had to choose one budget or the other. That made no sense to me, so I decided that the best way to sound the call for fiscal accountability was to get out in front on this. Keep in mind, it was a little unusual for a young congressman to go against the president of his own party on a budget proposal, and even more unusual when there didn't seem to be a whole lot of public support for a balanced budget, but I felt very strongly that we needed to make a fundamental change in this area, so I went out on my own little limb and hoped like crazy it could hold me.

That first year, the Bush budget received 213 votes on the House floor, out of a possible total of 435. The Democrats collected 230 votes for their rebuttal budget. We got a grand total of thirty votes for the Kasich budget, and I learned later that even some of the Democrats voted my way just so I could avoid a shellacking. They didn't want me to be completely embarrassed, but I was grateful for the few pity votes they threw my way.

That's how it goes when you take the lead. It can feel to you like you're a lone wolf howling on top of a mountain, but I believed my cause was just. And do you know what? Seventeen years later, I was one of the leading architects of the first balanced budget in a generation…proving to me yet again that sometimes you just have to keep howling.

Taking the lead means you'll have to face a whole lot more than the second-guessing of your home-town newspaper. Just look at the treatment of noted union organizer Crystal Lee Sutton, who in 1973 was fired from her job at the J.P. Stevens textile plant in North Carolina. Readers might know her as the in-spiration behind the movie *Norma Rae*, starring Sally Field, which told the story of a young textile worker-turned-activist who tried to organize a labor union in a fight for better wages and working conditions. For her efforts, Sutton was forcibly removed from the fac-tory floor by police—but not before she'd succeeded in building a groundswell of support among her fel-low workers.

When you're out in front—in a race, on an issue—it's not *just* the loneliest place on the planet. Too often, it can also be dangerous. Think back to some of the great leaders throughout our history, and you'll see evidence of this all around. We tend to lionize peo-ple like Martin Luther King, Jr., and rightly so, but in holding these folks on a pedestal we sometimes gloss over what it is they actually accomplished, what it is they were made to endure. Dr. King was fiercely devoted to his cause, and to the idea that he would not respond to violence with violence. Those around him were not to respond to violence with violence. And so, as a result of that pacifist approach to bringing about change, civil rights organizers were beaten and teargassed and jailed. Dr. King himself was jailed in Birmingham, where he wrote that famous letter in which he stated emphatically that "a just law is a man-made code that squares with the moral law or the law of God."

Dr. King went to jail for his beliefs. He suffered every criticism for his beliefs. He was threatened—and, indeed, he was ultimately killed for his beliefs.

Fannie Lou Hamer was another great civil rights activist who stood dangerously apart from consensus opinion. In her tireless, fearless efforts to register African American women in Mississippi—and, later, to recruit, train, and support *all* women of *all* races seeking election to public office—she was harassed, extorted, threatened, assaulted, and shot at by white supremacists...and even by local police, who attempted to keep her from exercising her right to vote.

And, still, she kept fighting the good fight... undaunted.

Before you start thinking it was easy for people like

Fannie Lou Hamer, Martin Luther King, Jr., and even Crystal Lee Sutton to make an impact because they were famous, let's remember that nobody knew who they were when they asked to be counted. Nobody knew the name Rosa Parks until she defiantly refused to give up her bus seat to a white passenger. These people became famous *because* of what they stood for, not the other way around.

Nelson Mandela epitomized what it meant to stand alone—and to raise the consciousness of the entire world in the process. Most of us are too young to remember when the anti-apartheid activist was first arrested and jailed for his beliefs, but the years of his confinement and his subsequent vindication as South Africa's president are etched on our hearts. His rousing 1964 speech in his own defense, in which he famously said of his anti-apartheid stance "it is an ideal for which I am prepared to die," signaled to the world that he would not be broken. My goodness, the man spent twenty-seven years in prison, often under horrific conditions (and, at one point, suffering from tuberculosis), but he was unwavering in his beliefs, and when apartheid was finally ended and Mandela appeared in that soccer stadium in Johannesburg before a crowd of a hundred thousand, alongside his wife, Winnie, we understood what it meant to lead.

What about the story of the human rights activist Natan Sharansky, who came to prominence as Anatoly Shcharansky, first as a child chess prodigy and later when he was famously held as a *refusenik* in Soviet prisons for over nine years? He wrote a book about his trial and imprisonment, *Fear No Evil*, in which he talked about how he used to always have a game of chess going in his head, against himself, to pass the time while in prison. That's the price a true leader must sometimes pay when he takes a principled stand—in this case, as a political prisoner.

I had the great honor of meeting Sharansky following his release, after I'd read his memoir, and I got to ask him about an especially moving passage in his book where he wrote about rejecting the KGB's latest offer of an early release if he would only recant his position and turn over the information they wanted. To persuade him, the Soviets compared his situation to Galileo, perhaps knowing that Sharansky believed him to be one of the true giants of history, but Sharansky would not use the scientist's name to justify what he would surely regard as his own moral failure.

Galileo had been excommunicated from the Catholic Church for the heresy of stating that the Earth orbited around the sun, but at first he would not bend what he knew about science and physics to suit prevailing public sentiments or a religious point of view—a moral imperative that still bears noting, by the way. In the end, however, he did recant, and conceded that the view of the church was correct after all.

Recall, they'd sent Sharansky to the gulag. I've never been in a Soviet labor camp so I can't even imagine the suffering this man was made to endure. I've read stories about it being so cold in the gulag that prisoners sleep next to the rats just to keep warm. But when his captors put it to him that all he had to do was recant and he would be released, Sharansky refused to do so.

"If I accepted the KGB's proposal," Sharansky wrote, "in addition to betraying myself I would be adding to the evil in the world. For perhaps at some future date my own decision would be a harmful influence on some other prisoner."

I told Sharansky that, for me, this was the most powerful part of the book, the essence of what it meant to stand for something—and to refuse to hide behind the good name or action of someone else.

As you probably know, the title of Sharansky's book

comes from Psalm 23, and it bears repeating here: "Though I walk through the valley of the shadow of death, I will fear no evil, for Thou art with me."

Another one of my personal heroes was William Wilberforce, who in the early 1800s took on the entire Parliament to abolish the slave trade. I talk about Wilberforce with my family all the time, so when they all went to London they made sure to visit the seated statue of him at Westminster Abbey. I wasn't with them on this trip, but my daughters took a picture of the statue for me because they understood how much this man's life meant to me. They knew how I'd been inspired by the way he stood against the mainstream in favor of what he knew to be right.

The Bible is fairly bursting with stories of leaders who walked their own lonely, often perilous roads— perhaps best exemplified in the story of Noah, who was tasked with building an ark in the middle of the desert in anticipation of a coming flood. The people thought he was some kind of madman, and yet Noah believed God was speaking to him, through him, and at His urging assembled all the animals of the world and marched them two by two onto this great vessel, on which he would sail with his family and ride out the coming storm that would wipe all evil from the face of the earth.

Here again, these Biblical and historical figures had yet to make history when they started out. Their impact was not yet known. But they started out anyway, and stood their ground, in ways that remind us you don't have to be famous in order to walk that lonely road and be successful. I repeat myself, I know, but it's an all-important point: it doesn't matter if you're fighting the school board to give your daughter an opportunity to play on the boys' football team, or trying to preserve a historic landmark that a popular local builder wants to raze to make way for a luxury housing project. It only matters that you put yourself out there and that you're prepared to take your licks.

Leadership comes in all shapes and sizes, but it almost always starts at home and grows from there—and, as often as not, it asks a whole lot from those out in front. As our leaders rise to meet their roles they tend to take on similar shape. In one way or another, at one point or another, they are all made to suffer the judgment of public opinion. They're all made to walk that lonely road for what can sometimes feel like an interminable stretch—to stand alone or apart before the rest of the world comes around.

Whether you're starting a movement, or simply standing firm in the face of injustice or uncertainty, you can expect to go it alone for a while. You can expect to take a whole lot of heat from those whose interests don't quite align with your own. But know this: as long as you have a clear idea where you're going and trust in your ability to get there, that lonely road will open up for you before long—and even if you take a wrong turn along the way, you'll have it in you to double back, dig deep, and continue the fight.

4

Slow Down

All truly great thoughts are conceived while walking.

—Friedrich Nietzsche

I don't know about you but my days are crammed with so much *stuff* I sometimes worry how I'll find the time to breathe. There's always something lining up for my attention, a long list of calls and emails I need to return, a pile of newspapers and magazines I mean to read, meetings I need to prepare for and attend, and it's tough to shut all of that off and get any kind of perspective or direction.

Now, I understand full well that a great many people are out there trying to get and keep ahead. Our workaday lives can be all-consuming. We're coming and going and moving every which way, pretty much all of the time. That's the reality we live in. Most folks, they believe that if they're not moving forward they're falling behind. They have no choice but to chase their paycheck. They've got student loans to repay, mortgages to service, mouths to feed. I *get* that—and believe me, I'm not looking to talk anyone down from that position. Trying to make ends meet puts a lot of us on an endless loop, where time always seems to be running out on us, and it starts to feel like we're going through the motions of living. Some of us are working two or three jobs just to keep our households going, and I'm not suggesting here that this *rush to solvency* isn't important—heck, it's vital.

But what's also vital is the need to step off the treadmill for a beat or two, every here and there. Let's call it a *rush to silence*—and let's agree to take a look at how we might dial down the heat and haste of our days. Much as we might think we need to fill every waking moment in a seemingly productive way, to keep moving full speed ahead, all out, all the time, in truth we all need to take a moment.

My great friend Tom Barrett, a clinical psychologist, has lately devoted much of his practice to the therapeutic benefits of slowing down. In the leadership training he offers, he helps clients reclaim a measure of control in their high-speed, high-stakes, high-stress lives. One of the ways he does this is by reminding them of the need to hold fast to what he calls the T3 Principle—Time to Think. "Without exception," he tells me, "when I talk to leaders around the world, I talk to them about this and get this involuntary flash of recognition. They all tell me it's so true. They need to learn to make that time, to distinguish between what needs their attention and what demands their attention."

One of the great metaphors Tom uses to explain the importance of mind management is to compare our bodies to a computer. "Our brains are like our software," he says, "and from time to time we need to do virus scans on them. We need to update them. We need to understand the system that's running the entire operation."

What this means, for a lot of us, is that we must make an extra effort to be alone with our thoughts. That can be hard. We should also find room in our days for friendships that have nothing to do with work, nothing to do with family, because these relationships offer us endless opportunities to unwind among like-minded souls. I know a great many people who are constantly moving and shaking, to the point where they can't bring themselves to sit still long enough to reflect on how their days are going. They don't have time for friends…they *barely* have time for family…and to them the idea of sitting in silence with nothing but their random thoughts to fill the time is plainly terrifying. Believe me, I know what it's like to feel unsettled when there aren't a million things going on, but I've come to realize the enormous riches to be found in reflection and quietude—because, let's face it, we are happier, healthier, friendlier, and more creative when we slow down.

It's tough for me to sit here and tell a single mother who gets up at five each morning to make breakfast, pack her kids' lunches, check their homework, and head out before the sun to punch the clock at the first of her two jobs that she ought to slow down. That's not the right message, is it? But what I *can* tell that single mom, and anyone else who's working so hard it feels like they're up against it, is that we can all find a point of pause in our days and steal a moment of quiet reflection.

We all need time to think, right? To consider…to *reconsider.*

Watch the grand masters play chess and you'll see that every move is carefully measured. The pace of play is very slow—it's remarkable to watch, especially if you understand the game, because the precise move is not always so apparent. Every once in a while they'll go on the clock, but for the most part they take the time to think a couple moves ahead, to plan their strategy, to weigh every possible scenario before moving forward. I'm not suggesting we live our lives in this methodical way, anticipating every possible outcome and defending ourselves from every conceivable line of attack, but there's something to be said for patience and deliberation. Sure, every once in a while we've got no choice but to be on the clock and follow our instincts, but our baseline tactic should be to take our time, to move with care and caution, to think through where we're going and how we mean to get there.

I'm trying to be better at this, but I haven't always practiced what I'm preaching here. For years, I was the guy trying to cram twenty-seven hours into a day— some days, I wouldn't even stop to eat lunch. Some decisions, I'd make with my gut instead of my head. But now that I've stepped away from public life, I'm making a conscious effort to make better choices with how I spend my time. One of the difficulties I had early on was learning to be a bit more disciplined in the invitations I accepted, the projects I took on. This was an adjustment. If an idea or initiative is interesting to me, or if I believe it's important, I'm inclined to want to throw in on it, but what I've learned is that this is not the best way to manage my time. I have to keep reminding myself of the safety instructions they give you on the plane before your flight takes off, when they tell you to take care of your own oxygen mask before assisting the child seated next to you. We need to set our best intentions aside and take care of ourselves before we can be of any use to those around us.

And so these days, more and more, I catch myself seeking opportunities for quiet reflection. Sometimes, it just happens—meaning, that I've been working at this in such a way that it's beginning to take hold. For example, I've noticed lately that I've become much more thoughtful in my actions. I'll set down my tablet or whatever it is I'm reading and just look out the window. I'll wait a beat or two before picking up my phone to return a call—maybe to think through what I want to say, or maybe just to set my mind at rest for another while. I'll notice that my shoulders are up and that I'm particularly tense, so I'll put down what I'm doing and stretch. Or go for a walk. I'll pick up the phone and call a friend I haven't spoken to in a while, or listen to a song I haven't heard in years, for no good reason other than it occurs to me to do so.

From time to time, I'll even listen to the sound of my own breath, and if you'd have told me a couple years ago that I'd be one of those people who listened to the sound of his own breath…well, I would have looked at you funny. One thing I hadn't realized, though, is that I'd been doing my own version of this sort of thing for most of my adult life—only, I never called it *quiet reflection*. I called it *golf*. For the longest time, golf has been my escape, my point of pause in my busy days, and when you're working on your golf game the way I'm always working on my golf game, you're taught to take the time to breathe before you take a shot. For whatever reason, I was never self-conscious about taking this kind of time in front of the other folks in my foursome—or even at the first tee box, where it can sometimes feel like the whole world is watching you.

But there I was, taking my time. Breathing. Not thinking. Totally in the moment…and now that I've come to think of my time on the course as a part of my meditative practice, I've begun to look forward to my next round all the more. The game absorbs all of my thinking, all of my distractions. It's an elixir. It's why my wife, Karen, never complains about the amount of time I spend on the golf course, because she knows it smooths out my edges and helps to make me a better person.

In my case, golf has always been one of those things, like work, that takes me away from my family. I've made time for the game, though, because the trade-off put it

in the win column for me—because the time I *did* spend
with my family was so much richer when I was relaxed
and my mind was clear. The game took the edges off
my day and kept me connected with my friends. Mostly,
it helped me to be totally engaged with my wife and
daughters on whatever we were doing as a family. In the
end, that's really what we're after here—slowing down
just enough that the time we do get to spend with the
people we love is more meaningful, more rewarding.

That said, simply being together under the same roof
isn't enough. That doesn't count as family time—not in
our house, anyway. One of the rules we put in place is
that there are no cell phones allowed at the dinner table.
A friend of mine had the great idea of setting up a charg-
ing station on a table by the front door, so that upon en-
tering the house everyone can park their phones there
and be free to interact with each other in a full-on way.
And yet even when we take these extra precautions, the
outside world has a tendency to find us. Every once in
a while, Mr. Hypocrite here reaches for his phone during dinner, and when that happens I catch some heat
for it, as I should. But I get it... I do. The idea is to shut
down these distractions for the next little while, so that
we can be more fully present for each other, and we
try to keep that rule going if we are having a meal at a

restaurant, or if one of my daughters and I stop for an ice-cream cone on our way home from some other activity. When we're together, we mean to be *together*—not pulled away from whatever's going on by a text or a phone call that can probably wait.

This togetherness thing is a big deal. I'm afraid it's missing in a lot of households these days. Everyone's on such a busy schedule, families don't even have time to sit down for an honest-to-goodness family dinner, so I think we'd all do well to make it a priority to coordinate our schedules and eat as a family at least a couple times each week. If a couple times a week sounds like a tall order, try to do it at least once each week. It's a far cry from the way a lot of folks from my generation grew up, where family dinners were a daily fact of life, but even just one night each week with full attendance and no distractions will begin to restore a feeling of connectedness that you might not have even realized has been lost.

And while you're at it, don't just stop at dinner. Watch a movie together as a family—even better, do a jigsaw puzzle, or play a board game, or start in on a home improvement project that everyone can handle. Whatever you're doing, find a way to power down your cell phones while you're in the middle of it, so that you can be fully present for each other, because it's when we carve out special pockets of time for our family and friends that we're better positioned to nourish these special relationships.

When we gift these stolen moments to ourselves, whether it's through a round of golf or a five-minute power nap, we can reenter our world in a more fully engaged way. When we come together with friends and family over an activity we can all enjoy, we can encourage the points of connection that nurture our relationships and ultimately sustain us. We can pay better attention to what's around us, what's expected of us. We can be present in a more meaningful way with the people we love.

Like I said, I fail at this, most of the time—or, at least, that's been the case until recently. During my public life, I didn't have the patience for this sort of thing. If I wasn't moving forward, I wasn't moving—that was my mindset. But I'm getting better at it. I'm realizing that I spend too much time filling my days with noise—phone calls that are unnecessary, material I don't need to read—and I find now that when I dial down that noise my interactions with people are richer, my energy level is greater, my thoughts are more focused. And it's because of all this that I'm able to be a better husband and father, a better friend and neighbor.

Think of it this way: as you slow down, you begin to see things you might miss at full throttle. It's like driving a car at high speed. You can't take in the passing scenery. Everything becomes a blur. You're not really looking at the trees, seeing the landscape you're traveling through. Or skiing down a mountain—same thing. You're whooshing by and failing to notice the majestic scenery all around. You're racing through the great outdoors but you're not experiencing the great outdoors.

It reminds me of that Kings of Leon song, "Waste a Moment," which tells us to take the time to do nothing much at all.

Even when it's our job to go fast we'll do well to slow down. I'm thinking here of my friend Bobby Rahal, the noted race car driver. I got to know Bobby in the late 1980s, after he'd won the Indianapolis 500. I was able to walk him into the Oval Office to be congratulated by a race car fan named Ronald Reagan, and we've stayed in touch ever since.

Bobby once told me he was at his best on the track when he took the time to gather his thoughts and catch his breath and make sure everything was working in synch. His fastest lap at the Indy came when he was able to control all the variables in preparing for the race and really focus on the path in front of him, while his slowest lap came when it felt to him like he had to hurry through his checklist and just hit the gas.

"You can't go racing into things all the time," he said—not the sort of thing you'd expect to hear from a race car driver. "You have to step back and see where you're going. I guess it's like when you get your life in the right place, with your family and your friends and your work. When all those things are aligned, life goes better, and things just run a little smoother, like a race car."

Yes, I guess this is so.

A lot of us, we're wired in such a way that we keep up our typical frantic pace even when we're on vacation. How crazy is *that*? You manage to set things up so you get a week off work and you arrange for a trip to Rome. It's the trip of a lifetime, right? But then you get there, and you're determined to see everything, all at once. You've lined up all these tours, and you're racing through the Vatican, and you get to the Sistine Chapel and you're worried about how much time you have before the next tour. Let me tell you something, if you're fortunate enough to visit the Sistine Chapel, you want to leave yourself time to take it all in. It's incredible. I've never been in a room that has so moved me, so inspired me—it's one of the wonders of the world, really. But it only resonates as a wonder if you take the time to wonder about it.

Art is like that. It's why we hold such a special place in our public trust for music and museums. For our public parks, too. Collectively, we've come to appreciate the need to step outside ourselves and take in another point of view, to listen to a song other than our own, to absorb the miracle of our open spaces, to reflect on those things that have true meaning in our lives. You don't have to be rich to do these things. You don't have to trek to the Himalayas to consider the meaning of life atop a great mountain. You can sit down on a park bench and watch the pigeons. You don't have to go all the way to Rome to see the miracle of Michelangelo's *The Last Judgment*. Maybe the miracle is hanging on your fridge—the finger-painting your child brought home from nursery school.

I heard a statistic the other day that troubled me. An administrator at one of the schools I visited told me that 40 percent of the students there were seeking counseling. I was there to give a speech, and the way it works a lot of the time is I get to take a little tour of the school beforehand, maybe meet some of the students and tap in to whatever's going on around campus. This administrator explained how the constant presence of tablet and laptop and smartphone screens has made it so students feel this tremendous pressure to keep plugged in at all times. Young people call it FOMO—fear of missing out—and it's a worrying thing. On the one hand, I hear a number like that from an educator and my first thought is how great it is that these kids are able to get the help they need in this area, but then I wonder if maybe the pressures to succeed or to keep up with everyone else wouldn't be mitigated somewhat if they simply slowed things down a couple notches and switched off those screens from time to time. They might miss out on someone's Instagram post, or maybe they'll be a little slower to discover some hot new restaurant or song that's got everybody's attention, but what they'll take in will be so much greater...so much *more*.

Here's another troubling statistic: the average individual has sixty thousand thoughts each day...and *90 percent* of them are negative. Ninety percent! What that tells me is we're spending far too much time on the things that drag us down and not nearly enough time on the things that might lift us up, so here we'll do well to accentuate the positive and find a way to quiet the noises that take us to these dark places.

I can't speak for other people. I won't presume to tell someone else they're moving too fast, or that their days are too full. But I do know this: when I stop what I'm

doing to look out my back window at the changing col-
ors of the trees in the woods behind my house...when
I set down the speech I'm writing and go for a short
walk...when I tell the folks I'm meeting with that we
can probably cover our agenda in a half-hour instead of
the forty-five minutes we've allotted on our schedules...
well, then I begin to see things in a whole new way. I'm
more attentive, more open to new ideas.

I'm *on it*, in a different way.

Look, we're all crazy busy. We have so many demands
on our time, so many challenges we're facing. We operate in make-or-break mode all the time—or, at least,
too much of the time. All I'm saying here is that if we
find a way to give ourselves a break, even if it's just the
tiniest sliver of a break, it will accrue to the good. Think
of it like a bank. For years, that's how I approached the
idea of exercise. Whenever I went to the gym, it's like I
was investing in my health and well-being. I was making a deposit, if you will. And if I couldn't make it to
the gym on any given day, I'd tell myself I was making
a withdrawal. It made me feel a little better about not
being able to get to the gym or the pool or wherever.
But you wouldn't visit your bank and make a withdrawal
every day without eventually making another deposit—
the math wouldn't work. So lately this has been my ap-

proach to claiming some reflective time throughout the day. I grab the time when I can, and trust that it will all add up to my benefit, as long as I don't draw down on my reserves.

Another way to think of it: the hectic pace of our days is like a glass of water freshly filled from the tap. You know how when there are all those air bubbles bouncing around in there and the water looks all cloudy? When you set the glass down for a moment and let the water be still, you'll see it starts to clear—that's what we're after here. We're seeking that still, quiet voice inside of us that gives us direction; that point of pause that allows us to consider a problem in a new way; that hobby that allows us to engage a different part of our brain. And it's not like we need to seek our little pieces of stillness in an isolated way. No, we can be still with our family, with our friends and neighbors, with our colleagues at work. Take the time in a meeting to ask the person across the table how they're doing—really ask how they're doing. Not how they're doing on this or that project or initiative, but in general. And be prepared to listen, because what you'll find when you give someone permission to open up to you is that there is strength in the sharing of our stories. Our problems are made smaller when we lean on others for support. Our victories are made richer.

Why do you think it is that when people talk about the bucket list of things they hope to do before they die that none of that stuff has anything to do with work? Twenty years ago, nobody was talking about their bucket list, but the concept has slipped into the culture in such a way that it speaks to this idea that we're all somehow putting off what we really want to be doing in favor of what we think we should be doing. Everybody's list is about *I would like to see this*—or *I would like to go there*. It's about the things we hope to do or find or discover beyond our everyday experiences. It's never about needing to work longer hours or taking on more responsibilities. Personally, I'm not a fan of the term or the time-is-running-out concept behind it, but there's no denying the power it has come to hold on a societal level. We've set it up so it's this far-off fantasy, a to-do list of things we're too busy *to do*...but we need to find a way to tap into the spirit of these bucket lists in whatever ways we can.

Step outside yourself, pull back, power down—in whatever ways make sense for you and your situation. Make it a goal to find some time that's just for you and see what happens.

5

Bounce Back

Do not judge me by my success, judge me by how many times I fell down and got back up again.

—Nelson Mandela

Resilience.

It's the ability to recover from a disappointment or difficulty. The will it takes to keep pressing when all appears lost. The strength to persevere. Some of our setbacks can be devastating, of course, and some are merely dispiriting, but the ways we stand back up when we fall will come to define us over time.

In my own life, I think of that terrible night in August 1987 when my parents were killed in a car accident. I was a young congressman, shuttling between Washington and Columbus, trying to make the world a better place, trying to make my parents proud. Then I got this call with devastating news. It's everybody's nightmare, right? It brought me back to the fear I used to have as a child, whenever my father went to pick up my mother from work and I worried they wouldn't come home—and now, all these years later, that fear came to pass.

I've written about this sad chapter before, so I don't want to dwell on it here except to point out that at the time I didn't think I would ever recover from the loss, and for a long while there I couldn't see how I'd ever fight my way back to whole. Happily, with the help of my faith and many enduring friendships, I found myself again, and I continue to find joy and meaning in my life.

Over the next thirty-plus years, most of them in public life, I was made keenly aware of the very many ways we suffer and struggle: addiction, job loss, estrangement from family, poverty, depression, injury, and health issues...there's no end to the burdens we all share. And yet I've come to realize that things are never quite as bad as they first appear, and that even the biggest problems in our lives can be brought down to manageable size with patience, perspective, and resolve.

For every darkness, there is a light—we must sim-

ply keep our heads up and our eyes open to see what
we can see.

I don't mean to soft-pedal the very real pain we
are sometimes made to endure by suggesting that the
pain will simply pass. Time is an essential salve, but
it's not about waiting out the pain until it goes away as
much as it is finding a way to rise above it. This goes
for our somewhat lesser pains as well—you know, the
small defeats that find us on a day-to-day basis, like
getting passed over for a promotion, or scrambling
to get home to your family after your flight has been
canceled. Resilience comes in all shapes and sizes, but
be assured, we can be pretty durable. A lot of times,
you'll find out that a disappointment in one area might
lead to an unexpected opportunity in another. That
promotion that didn't come your way? It might push
you to consider an entirely new line of work, where
you were really meant to be all along.

It takes a whole lot to kill the human spirit, I've
come to realize, and one of the good things that attached to that dark time in my life after my parents
were killed was my ability to connect with people
who were going through dark times of their own.
And it wasn't just my *ability* in this regard, it was my
responsibility as well—this, too, came into full focus. In

my renewed sense of faith there was a renewed sense of belonging, and over the years I've taken it upon myself to reach out to those who might be stumbling or hurting in some way.

This may or may not have been a good thing. It depends who you ask. My wife tells me I sometimes stick my nose where it doesn't belong, and I suppose this is true, but I do it anyway. For example, Karen and I have a friend who suffers from depression. She doesn't like to talk about it, but when we saw her at a party I took her aside and pushed her to do just that. In the moment, it wasn't entirely clear that this woman welcomed the conversation, but I pressed her to talk just the same. I asked her how she was faring and in the long pause that followed while she tried to formulate an answer I could tell she was in a desperate place.

I said, "Do you think you can make it through the year?"

She said she wasn't sure.

I said, "What about the next six months?"

Again, she couldn't say.

I said, "What about the next month?"

Just then, a month to her seemed like forever.

Finally, I said, "How 'bout the next week? Can you make it through the next week?"

A week, she could handle…and she said as much and we moved on from there. Somehow, with this short-term objective laid out in front of my dear friend, the weight of her days didn't seem so suffocating or terrifying, and she was able to claw her way out of it and get back to the business of living…at least, for the next while. I know this because I made it a special point to check in on her from time to time, and she told me she appreciated my concern. She even reached back out to say she was doing much better— certainly not because of me, or anything I might have said or done, but I was happy for her that her days were looking brighter.

Setbacks are inevitable in this life, and while I wouldn't go so far as to suggest we ought to welcome them, we should take comfort in knowing that we can overcome them. We can…we *must*. Admittedly, we sometimes need a little bit of help in this area, and this can lead us to one of the great side benefits of a regret or a sadness of some kind: they open us up to the kindness and support of others. One of our most underutilized strengths, I've come to believe, is our ability to ask for help, to open ourselves up and admit we're hurting and in need of support, because it takes a certain grit to acknowledge our weaknesses and ask for help. With me, when I lost my parents, that support came initially from a minister who steered me back to a life of faith, a life I had momentarily set aside. With others, relief comes from sharing their burdens with those who've gone through a similar ordeal.

A powerful example of this is the community of caring my friend Tim Bainbridge was able to access when his wife was diagnosed with Alzheimer's. Tim's been a member of our Bible study group for over ten years, so I knew he was hurting over his wife's illness. There were resources in place to help Tim manage her care, but it wasn't until he sought out a support group for caregivers like himself that Tim was able to focus on his own health and well-being, and to hear him tell it the group has given him great comfort and up-lift. Let us not forget, there is safety in numbers, and here Tim was able to share his grief and his difficul-ties with others who were also hurting in a similar way. It's been a godsend, really—in fact, Tim made such a deep connection with a woman in the group who was losing her husband to the disease that the two new friends got together after they'd lost their partners and decided to become engaged.

How about *that*?

Tim's story, like mine following the deaths of my

parents, offers an extreme example of the ways a tragedy can derail us, and the affirming ways faith and friendship can restore us, but I see the power of resilience every day as I travel the country. I see young adults struggling with drug addiction who somehow manage to make it to a substance abuse program and turn their lives around. I see parents doing their best to raise a child with autism and discovering the strength they need to celebrate the hard-won triumphs they find along the way. I see athletes, in huge arenas and in small-town high school gyms, picking themselves up after a horrifying injury and battling back to resume their careers. I see every imaginable display of grit and fortitude and indomitable strength, and some unimaginable ones besides.

How about the young man from Brunswick, Georgia, who didn't miss a single day of school for thirteen years? Talk about resilience! Alex Kunda was only four when his older sister Miranda died from a debilitating illness known as autoimmune hepatitis, but before she passed he made a promise to her that he'd never miss a day of school. The promise reminded Alex to make the most of his life, even in the face of such extreme sadness, and he kept to it…all the way from kindergarten to the last day of his senior year in high school.

"This was the one promise I remembered making to her," he told a CBS News reporter who turned up to cover this stirring story. "And I can't make any more promises to her in person, anymore. So the one promise I did make, I was going to keep it."

What's interesting about Alex's resolve was that for a while his parents wanted to pull him out of school to take some of the pressure off of his perfect attendance record. They worried that he was pushing himself to go to school when he was sick, and that the longer he kept his string going the harder it would be to miss a day later on, so when he was in the third grade they arranged to pull him out of school one Friday afternoon so the family could take a weekend trip to Disney World. Alex, true to his word, refused to skip school, even for the chance to see Mickey and Minnie—that's how determined this young man was to power past his grief and honor his sister's memory in this way.

Resilience needs a guiding hand, don't you think? That's why we see athletes reach down to help up an opponent who might have fallen on the last play, why colleagues might lift each other up after a tough slog at work. And then of course there's the garden-variety resilience we all need to tap that has nothing to do with grief or depression or injury. There's the deep well of regret that often finds us when we fall short of a long-held goal. Or the soft fall of disappointment when things simply don't go our way. What happens when you set out to achieve something at work or in your personal life—something you really want, something you believe you really deserve—and it remains just out of reach? Sometimes willing it and working for it can't quite make it so, which leaves you with a couple options. You can either pick yourself up and go at it again—perhaps with a slightly different strategy or approach—or you can set your sights on another objective. If a door has been closed to you at work, you can try beating it down and hoping it will finally open up for you, but at some point you might realize it's an exercise in futility. After all, it's one thing to be resilient, and quite another to fool yourself into thinking absolutely anything is possible.

When you don't get what you want in this life, it doesn't mean you should allow yourself to be cast as a victim. It only means that you need to try a new approach—or, perhaps, recalibrate your dreams and consider some of the reasons you might have fallen short the first time around.

Resilience also speaks to our ability to change with the times. I saw a statistic recently that said today's college graduates will hold approximately eight different full-time jobs before they retire—a long cry from my parents' generation, when most people we knew stayed at one company their entire working lives. What's acutely concerning to our young people are the jobs that are disappearing on the back of our changing technology. Consider the trucking industry: if you're a truck driver today, it's more than likely that you won't be a truck driver tomorrow. For all the advantages they promise, autonomous, self-driving vehicles are going to put a whole lot of truckers out of work, and if you drive for a living you need to be aware of that, and you need to be resilient and nimble enough to shift gears. You can't just wave a white flag and call it a career. You need to be talking to your employer, to see what this new technology might mean for your future with the company. You need to tap into any retraining programs they might be offering, or go out on your own and prepare yourself to meet the changes ahead.

The truck driver who sits and fumes and does nothing to address his or her own situation will be the one without the job; the one who prepares for the revolution to come will find a way to drive into the future.

Remember Jim Ryun, the great American miler?

I served with him for a stretch in Congress, where he represented his home district in Kansas, and got to know him pretty well. But let's be clear, I knew him by reputation before I met him in Washington, and it's that reputation I want to spend some time talking about here. As a high school junior, Jim Ryun became the first high school athlete to break the four-minute barrier in the mile. As a senior, he set a schoolboy record in the mile that stood for almost forty years. Before he graduated, at the age of seventeen, he participated in the 1964 Olympics in Tokyo, and he made the Olympic team again in 1968, when he was expected to win the 1,500 meters in Mexico City. Trouble was, nobody told Kip Keino, the legendary distance runner from Kenya. At the finish, Jim came up a couple seconds short, earning the silver medal to Kip Keino's gold, and a lot of folks were disappointed. To Jim's great credit, though, he wasn't one of them. He'd run the race of his life, and actually ran faster than he ever dreamed, but the Kenyan was too tough for him to beat at altitude.

Jim came back four years later, for the Munich Games, expecting to finally win his gold medal— that's resilience of a kind, yes? He'd been posting some of the best times of his life, had been training with dogged determination, only here he was tripped during one of the qualifying heats. His coach had always taught him that if he ever fell, his one and only job was to get right back up and keep running. It was drilled into him. So that's what he did, but he was too far back to make up the ground he'd lost and he failed to advance to the finals—calling for resilience of an extra special kind.

The image of Jim Ryun, America's hope in those Games, the youngest American male to ever qualify for the US Olympic track team, lying flat on his back for those few long beats and picking himself up and continuing on to the finish line…well, it was one of the most enduring, most uplifting images in all of sports, and I carried it with me for the longest time. Think about *that*: all had clearly been lost, but instead of burying his face in his hands and despairing he kept running, off in pursuit of a goal he would now never reach. There was something terrifically inspiring about the way Jim got back up and continued running, shouldering his obvious disappointment, and when I asked him about it years later he shared that there was inspiration in that moment for him, as well. As he left the track that day after the race and walked through the tunnel beneath the stadium to the locker room, he said he found his higher purpose. Together with his wife, he resolved right there in Munich that his life would not end with that one spill onto the track. He might have lost the race, and what would turn out to be his last chance at a gold medal, but he still had the race of his life left to run, and he would run with the Lord the rest of the way.

I've often thought about what it takes to step away from a regret or a difficulty, and long admired folks like Jim who are able to do so with grace. And then there are those folks without an ounce of quit in them, and without that support team in place to tell them it's time to move on—that's *persistence*, really, a kissing cousin to *resilience*, and it takes me in a sidelong way to the 2016 presidential campaign, so as long as I'm on it I'll offer this: I didn't seek the Republican nomination for president *just* to be the second-to-last candidate standing in that crowded field of hopefuls. No, I was in it to win it, and I gave it my all, but at some point the math and the calendar were lined up against me in such a way that winning was no longer a prospect. So what did I do? I went back to the business of being governor of the great state of Ohio, which I'd said all along was one of the best jobs in the world, and I contented myself with the many blessings that flowed my way from the campaign. I might not have won the nomination, but I'd been gifted a tremendous opportunity to share my hopes and dreams with the American people. I got to talk at length about the issues and values that mattered to me—issues and values that I thought were important for us all to consider. And I got to make a deeply personal connection with countless numbers of fine, hardworking folks who responded to the positive messages I tried to put out there—and who in turn went back into their own communities, inspired to share those positive messages.

Oh, I was disappointed that I wasn't able to take my campaign all the way to the Republican National Convention. I ran for president because I thought I'd do a good job, and because I thought I was uniquely qualified, and when it didn't work out I returned to my life at home in Ohio and counted the many blessings that came along with *that*. How many times does it happen that we strive for a goal, or a promotion at work, or some exciting new opportunity, and then when it doesn't happen we look back in our rearview mirror and tell ourselves that what happened for us instead was so much better? Well, the 2016 campaign wasn't quite like that for me, but there were silver linings all around—primarily, the rich and wonderful connections I was able to make with voters and supporters all across the country. Plus, once I was off the campaign trail and headed for home, I contented myself with the fact that I'd now have so much more time to spend with my twin teenage daughters before they left for college, presuming they even wanted their old man around.

The campaign itself was a lesson in resilience. Early on, following a second-place showing in the New Hampshire primary, we suffered some devastating losses, but we hung in there as a team. We picked each other up. There were times when someone on my campaign team would rally the troops and lift our collective spirits, and there were other times when the rallying fell to me. We took turns supporting each other, and reminding each other that we couldn't let down our volunteers, or the people of Ohio, or the voters who'd already honored us with their votes.

Over time, I began to see that the campaign was like any other endeavor, any other enduring relationship, any other workplace environment. We had our good days and our bad days. When things appeared bleak, something good would happen to brighten our prospects. When we were riding high, we'd hit a trouble spot and wonder how we ever thought we could take this thing all the way to the convention. Somewhere in there we were all made to realize that resilience doesn't happen without a little bit of help. You need people around you to cheer you on, to remind you that your goal is within reach. Or, maybe you need them to be straight with you and let you know you're reaching just a little above your pay grade and that it's not likely to happen for you in the ways you imagine—that message is important, too. It might be tough to hear, but it's essential if we mean to move ourselves forward.

Here I was lucky enough to have my friends and supporters in agreement: we'd all given it our best shot, but it was time to move on to the next challenge.

6

Love Thy Neighbor

The best and most beautiful things in the world cannot be seen or even touched. They must be felt with the heart.

—Helen Keller

Has it ever felt to you like kindness is a dwindling commodity? Simple, basic human kindness—we don't see as much of it as we used to, perhaps, and we certainly don't see as much of it as we'd like, but when we *do* see it...you better believe it makes an impression. It does. It brings us together, and reminds us of the ways we're connected, so I want to spend some time on this, and see if there's maybe some way we can *all* do a little better when it comes to how we make time for each other.

Kindness takes many forms. It finds us in acts of selflessness and sacrifice, and in small shows of concern, and it makes a particular impression when we see one of these generous impulses in our children. As governor, I used to give out Courage Awards to Ohioans who were doing good, helping out in their communities, overcoming hardships in such a way that they were able to inspire others. It was one of my favorite events of the year—and one of my greatest blessings as governor to be able to honor these good people in this way. The youngest recipient during my tenure was a nine-year-old boy named Mikah Frye. Like a lot of kids, Mikah wanted an Xbox gaming system for Christmas, but Mikah's story was a little unusual. He'd been raised by drug-addicted parents, been in and out of homeless shelters. He'd been bullied at school. The poor kid had had a tough road, so when he was finally settled and living with his grandmother he let it be known that this was something he wanted. But then he had another thought. Mikah told his grandmother she should take the three hundred dollars it would cost for an Xbox and use the money instead to buy blankets for the homeless. He knew what it was like to be in one of those shelters on a cold night. He knew that even if you were lucky enough to be handed a blanket one night, you'd have to give it back in the morning and never know if you'd get another one. He knew three hundred dollars could buy a whole bunch of blankets, and he thought it would be great to present a few people with a blanket they could actually keep, so his grandmother helped to make that happen.

Mikah's generosity could go only so far, but people heard about it and his Ashland neighbors started taking up the cause, helping to lead an ongoing effort to help the homeless in the area. After a while, donations started coming in from all across the country, which was a tremendous thing to see. Also tremendous: somebody heard about Mikah's kindness and sent him that Xbox he'd been eyeing at the beginning of all of this, reminding us that even though kindness is its own reward, this paying it forward business can sometimes hit you on the rebound.

Kindness also comes in a generosity of spirit, and here I'm thinking of a story I saw on *CBS News Sunday Morning* about an eighty-year-old widow from Oxford, Alabama, named Eleanor Baker. Eleanor lives alone with her dog. She's pretty self-sufficient, though, and she likes to go out to eat from time to time, and she's gotten used to dining alone. That's one of the sad facts of life when you get a little bit older—maybe your spouse is no longer around, or your family has moved out of town, and you're forced to learn how to keep yourself company.

Well, one night Eleanor walked into Brad's Bar-B-Que, a favorite local joint, and she sat down at a table for one. Across the way sat three young men, all in their twenties, and one of them noticed Eleanor sitting all by herself, so he got up and approached her table to say hello.

He said, "Do you mind having some company?"

The young man's name was Jamario Howard, and at Eleanor's invitation he and his two friends joined her for dinner, and when they were finished they realized they'd all had such a marvelous time they made plans to get together again.

"I already feel like we're her grandkids," Jamario told the reporter.

He also said this: "I want to change the world somehow. And I don't know how. I'm not rich. I'm not famous. And I'm not very smart either, so I can't be president. But we can show the world it's alright to be kind. And then, before long, maybe the world will be a much better place."

Yes, Jamario, it's alright to be kind. In fact, it's more than alright—it's essential.

We need to make time for each other. Just how to

quantify this, I've got no idea, except to say that whatever it is you're now doing, you need to be doing a whole lot more. *We* need to be doing a whole lot more. We need to care for each other, love each other... *acknowledge* each other. Remember, it's the little things that count in the biggest way. We should all be taking the time to show a simple kindness to our friends and neighbors, even to perfect strangers like Eleanor Baker. If you see someone dining alone, invite them to join you. If you see someone down, lift them up. If you see darkness, be the light. You'll be surprised at the riches that'll come your way on the back of the small, sweet gestures you put out into the world, so go ahead and help someone load their car in the supermarket parking lot, or check in with that relative you've always been meaning to call. And if you notice one of your friends celebrating a milestone or a special accomplishment on social media, think about picking up the phone to offer your congratulations instead of just "liking" or commenting online.

We should never underestimate the importance of good company—for some, it can be an all-important lifeline, as it is for the singer-songwriter Anders Osborne, a recovering alcoholic. Anders started an organization called "Send Me A Friend," to help sober artists like himself to continue to work in and around the bar and festival music scene, where drinking is a part of the culture. He got the name from the title of one of his songs. The way it works, if you're a musician traveling to an unfamiliar town, is that you can tap into a network of local volunteers who'll come out to support you and keep you company while you're on the road.

"It's all about going back to work," Anders told NPR, when news of his outreach in this area started to spread. "It's not about getting anybody sober. That's not my job. It's just, if you have chosen not to drink or drug anymore but you want to stay in the music industry…well, we're going to provide one small little service, which is, we're going to send somebody out to sit there with you."

Sometimes that's all it takes to make a difference, just being there for somebody. And, listening. One of the things that sets me off is when people ask you how you're doing and don't even stop to hear the answer. I've been guilty of doing the same thing, but when I do take the time to look people in the eyes and really *listen* to what they have to say on this, it can put a nice little exclamation point on my day…and, hopefully, on their day, as well. There's a manager at my club who's especially good at this. His name is Doug Sadler, and he certainly deserves a shout-out here because he gives you his full attention when he greets you—and if he misses you on the way in, he'll circle back and find you before long, just to say hello and make you feel welcome.

I told Doug one day how impressed I was by his genuine attentiveness, and he just kind of shrugged me off, saying, "Well, Governor, if I ask you how you're doing I ought to at least listen to the answer."

He's right about that—and yet it's so rare (and refreshing!) when you come across someone who takes this kind of thing seriously.

Looking out for others isn't *just* about being helpful or friendly or attentive. It also involves sacrifice—often, great sacrifice. Let's say you're at a concert in Las Vegas, a country music festival. All of a sudden you start to hear shots firing out, only you don't recognize the sounds as gunfire at first because it's just so incongruous. You're out with your friends, having fun, dancing...the last thing in the world you imagine is a hail of gunfire, but there it is. *Here* it is, and you're right in the middle of it. There's blood everywhere, but then someone you've never met throws his body over yours to protect you. He doesn't stop to ask if you are a Democrat or Republican. He doesn't even stop to ask your name. He's just one human being trying to help another human being in a desperate situation.

Let me tell you, the stories that came out of that tragic shooting on the Las Vegas Strip on the night of October 1, 2017—the deadliest mass shooting in US history, leaving fifty-eight people dead and 422 wounded—are beyond belief, beyond inspiring. There were so many heroes on those concert grounds that night, and I'm afraid some of those heroes were taken from us as well, but their sacrifices show us the best of who we are, and what I can't shake thinking about all this time later is how these heroic acts were instinctive. These good people didn't have to think about what they were doing, they just did what needed to be done, and here I think we have to acknowledge that while most of us might have the instinct to do good there are some of us who are capable of great evil.

And keep in mind, these folks were not anonymous. Their selfless heroism did not go unnoticed. In fact, there was at least one Ohio woman on the scene—a hospice nurse from Miamisburg named Chris Hole— who bravely ran to tend to the injured and fallen as the hail of gunfire continued all around her, helping to stanch their wounds and ferry them to waiting vehicles for transport to the nearest hospital. We honored her with a 2018 Courage Award, and learned firsthand what it was like to be in the middle of that kind of chaos, being thrown to the ground, and cut and bruised by everyone attempting to flee the scene, even as she was rushing in to help those in need.

Sadly, the spate of gun violence in twenty-first-century America has given us way too many opportunities for this type of extreme selflessness. I'm still trying to get my head around the supreme sacrifice of a young man named Riley Howell, who charged a gunman in his University of North Carolina classroom and pinned him down until law enforcement arrived on the scene. In the tragic aftermath of that attack on April 30, 2019, Charlotte police credited Riley with preventing an untold, unimaginable number of casualties.

The attack claimed the lives of two students, including Riley, and injured four others.

"He is my hero," Riley's longtime girlfriend, Lauren Westmoreland, told a *New York Times* reporter who was doing a follow-up story on the shooting. "But he's just my angel now, as well."

Just one week later, a young man named Kendrick Castillo threw *himself* into the line of fire to thwart the attack of another shooter at the STEM School Highlands Ranch, in Colorado, helping to save another untold number of lives.

Kendrick was the only student killed in this attack, which injured eight others.

Sometimes, the life-and-death bravery of our heroes involves a different measure of sacrifice. Michael Phelps was already a hero of a kind after winning all those Olympic swimming medals, but he deserves a whole other set of medals for the way he started speaking out on the issue of mental illness. Have you seen those public service ads he's been doing? He's sitting at the bottom of the pool on a chair, talking about how he's spent most of his life looking down—because, hey, that's what swimmers see when they're doing their laps. Then he says he should have been spending more time looking up and out at the world around, and paying better attention to the people in his life.

While I'm on the subject of mental health, I want to tell you about University of Virginia junior Kyle Guy. If you follow college basketball, you'll remember Kyle as the young man who calmly stepped to the free throw line with less than a second to go in the semifinal game of the NCAA tournament. His team was down 62–60, and all eyes were on him—over seventy thousand pairs of them at US Bank Stadium in Minneapolis, not to mention the eyes of the basketball world. As big moments go, this one was pretty grand. Kyle had been fouled on a three-point attempt, so if he hit all three foul shots he'd send his team to the NCAA finals.

Now that's pressure!

Before the tournament, Kyle had spoken publicly about the anxiety issues he'd faced his entire life. Those issues had come to the surface in a very chilling, very public way after Virginia was eliminated in the first round of the 2018 tournament in a shocking upset that left Kyle questioning his commitment to the game. He'd already struggled with his anxiety before the upset loss, but now his dark moments were even darker. He struggled away from the gym, and with the encouragement of his family, his friends, and his coaches, he sought help. He'd posted about his difficulties on Facebook. He was already a hero to many for his brave honesty—but then, when he hit those three free throws and Virginia won the game 63–62, he became a hero to so many more because when he had our full attention during all those postgame interviews, he talked about this stuff some more. He talked about how he used to cry at practice, or in the locker room, because he felt so all alone. He talked about the dark, desperate places he'd been in his mind. And then, after Virginia went on to win the national championship and Kyle was named the MVP of the tournament, he said something remarkable. He talked about how it was great to win a championship, but allowed that the bigger blessing was the chance to be a beacon of light for others walking in the darkness of depression.

"That means more to me than anything I could ever do on the basketball court," he told a *USA Today* reporter after the game, "to be able to help someone who is suffering."

You know, when I first saw Kyle being interviewed during the tournament, I thought to share his story in the previous chapter on resilience—because, really, his triumph was a testament to his hard work and conviction. There was just no quit to this guy, even in his darkest, most desperate moments. Where others might have seen weakness, there was only strength. But then I thought about it some more and realized his story was a better fit here, in a discussion on using your gifts in service of others. Helping out, extending a kindness, *showing up*…it's the essence of who we are as human beings, and it gets me every time.

Did you see the smile on the face of Sofia Sanchez, a little girl from Chicago in need of a heart transplant who got a chance to meet her idol just before her surgery? Sofia posted a video of herself tethered to an IV dancing down a hospital hallway to Drake's "In My Feelings." In the caption accompanying her video, Sofia invited Drake to her eleventh birthday party, to be held in her hospital room the following week.

Sure enough, Drake showed up at the party, and the footage from that moment when he walked into Sofia's room and her face lit up was about as life-affirming as it gets—go ahead and Google it and see for yourself.

"You asked me to come," Drake said. "I'm here."

That's really what it comes down to, in the end. Showing up for each other. Being there for each other. Doing for each other.

When your friend finds out her mother's been diagnosed with breast cancer, do you make the time to cry with her?

When your roommate aces her final exam, do you celebrate with her?

When your coworker needs a ride home from work because her car's in the shop and the bus drops her off more than two miles from where she lives, do you take her?

My thing is to call people. I may have my flaws and my failings, but one thing I'm good at is getting on the phone and checking in with folks—sometimes, for no reason other than to just say hello. I'll call people when they're sick, or struggling. I'll call them a couple weeks after the loss of a loved one, just to let them know I'm thinking about them.

When I was governor, there was a guy in my cabinet who'd just had major surgery—let's call him Pete, since I don't want to step on his privacy by sharing this story. At one point, following one of our staff meetings, I asked if anyone had called Pete to see how he was doing. One person said they didn't want to bother him. Another person said that if something was going on with Pete we would have surely heard about it. And another said he'd posted something online he was hoping Pete might see.

Like I've said throughout the book, I don't always do right by the people closest to me, but I try—and this right here was kind of in my wheelhouse: I call people… I reach out. So I lit into these folks and said, "You don't want to bother him? Why not let Pete decide if he wants to hear from you? If he doesn't want to take the call, he won't answer."

Frankly, we don't always know what to say when people are having a hard time, but what I've learned over the years is that it doesn't really matter what you say—it only matters that you let them know you're there. When you look at it this way, it's the easiest thing in the world to call someone like Pete and say, "Hey, I don't want to bother you, I just want you to know I'm thinking about you and wish you the best."

That's all.

When you get into the habit of reaching out in this way, you might find it's contagious. A couple hours after this exchange about Pete's surgery, one of the staffers who'd been in that meeting with me asked me if I'd heard the news about another one of our colleagues—let's call him Steve. She said, "I'm bringing this up because of what you said about Pete," so there was this wonderful ripple effect happening in our office, with people suddenly paying good and close attention to each other, and here this staffer wanted me to know that Steve had just been diagnosed with pancreatic cancer, so we all took turns checking in with him, as well.

Another one of my things, apparently, is hugging. I'd never thought of myself as a hugger of any size or stripe, but during the 2016 presidential campaign I had a couple folks open up to me in such a way at my town halls that a certain amount of hugging was inevitable—a happy by-product of the warmth and good feelings that tended to find us at a number of these meetings. For whatever reason, when the conversation turned away from taxes and immigration and foreign policy, I was able to get voters to open up to me about some of their personal challenges—and in that kind of welcoming, nurturing environment… well, what else could we do but hug it out?

It actually happened a bunch of times during the campaign, once people started to see that I cared about them and the future we might build together, but there was one hug in particular that got a whole lot of attention. I was at a town hall event at Clemson University, when a young man showed up and started talking about some of the issues affecting his family. We had a nice little exchange, and when it was over the young man asked if I would give him a hug. So I walked off the stage and gave him the best hug I could muster, and when we broke our embrace he noticed I was crying, and the country noticed it, too. People talked about it for a while. I still get asked about it from time to time—and when that happens, as often as not, the person doing the asking might request a hug of their own. If the moment doesn't seem too awkward or squishy or inappropriate to the situation, I'll try to comply—because, hey, it's the least I can do.

7

Get Out of Your Silo

Your assumptions are your windows on the world. Scrub them off every once in a while, or the light won't come in.

—Isaac Asimov

When you break it down, a lot of what's wrong with the ways we communicate with each other has to do with the ways we take in our news and information. When I was growing up, Americans tuned in to watch the nightly news on one of the three major networks, and in most of our midsize to major cities there were at least two daily newspapers providing what many felt was objective reporting and helpful analysis. These days we catch snippets of the news when we can, in bits and bytes, without really stopping to think about where the information is coming from or how it was gathered.

Perhaps the most concerning development in how

we keep informed is the tendency we all have to seek out news outlets that affirm what we already know— or, I should say, what we *think* we already know. In a lot of ways, we've come full circle from the heyday of print journalism in cities like New York where there were more than a dozen daily newspapers, published in morning and afternoon editions, each with a dedicated readership, each with a distinct point of view. I don't mean to mix my mediums, but nobody called it *narrowcasting* back then, even though there was a definite bias of the kind we see today with the fracturing of our news media.

About that: it sometimes seems we're all entrenched in our own media silos, taking in only the information we want to hear, and I'm afraid the result of all this *narrowcasting* is a society doomed to *narrowthinking*. Think about it: if we only seek out news and information likely to support our predisposed points of view…if we're determined to only take in opinions that confirm or somehow justify the opinions we already have…well, then our national conversation can never really get started.

Over thirty years ago, the philosopher Allan Bloom wrote a bestselling book called *The Closing of the American Mind*, about what he saw as the failure of higher education to reflect the changing mores of the times, and I've lately been thinking the title can be repurposed to address the ways we seem to want to close ourselves off from opinions other than our own. Social media hasn't really helped. On the one hand, the internet has offered easy and boundless access to every conceivable bit of news and information—and some *inconceivable* ones, as well. On its face, this is a good and wondrous thing, but the flip side to all those points of connection is that there are no checks and balances in place to help us distinguish truth from fiction, news from propaganda, or objective criticism from slander. The net effect, in many ways, has been to push people into their own corners, encouraging them to double down in their beliefs and ratchet up their own efforts to disseminate slanted accounts and questionable analysis that echo their own deeply held points of view.

A lot of people call social media the "fifth estate," for the way it stands as a kind of informal corollary to the "fourth estate" of the press. In case you're wondering, the terms come from the European ideal of the three estates of the realm: the clergy, the nobility, and the commoners. The American interpretation of this concept can be seen in our three branches of government: the legislature, the executive branch, and the judiciary. Traditionally, the fourth estate of the press has stood outside the framework of our political system and served as a kind of watchdog, and it's been under attack of late. Our press freedom is one of the great bulwarks of our democracy, and we should be out there building it up and supporting it instead of knocking it down and questioning it, but that's a whole other conversation.

For *this* conversation, let's keep the focus on the changes we've seen in our media landscape in recent years. In our electronic age, the government was able to regulate our broadcast media because the government controlled our airwaves. You needed a license to be able to operate, and along with that license you were expected to report objectively on the issues of the day, giving equal voice to opposing points of view. That standard of objectivity seemed to attach to our most influential daily newspapers and national magazines as well, where fair and balanced reporting has always been prized.

In our digital age, these standards seem to have disappeared. When I was on the campaign trail, I sometimes compared social media to the Wild West because it's as if anything goes. There are fringe media outlets and lone-wolf podcasters and even basic cable channels offering their own takes on the news of the day without constraint. There often appears to be no such thing as equal time or fair and balanced reporting—only the bottom-line goal to attract as many eyeballs or earbuds as possible. Meanwhile, viewership has been dwindling at our broadcast networks over the past several decades, where the ideal of fair and balanced reporting is still prized. The nightly news no longer occupies our national attention in quite the same way—there are just too many ways for people to get and keep informed. On the print side, the daily news holes in our major daily newspapers are shrinking, and magazines are moving more and more to online publishing models that seem to be leaving an entire generation of older Americans without their accustomed ways of keeping informed, while an entire generation of younger Americans has come of age without ever really getting in the habit of reading a comprehensive, thoroughgoing news account.

I'm not pointing fingers here, or suggesting that the media is doing anything wrong. It's just that the landscape has changed. The *transaction* has changed—meaning, the deal we make with ourselves before deciding if a piece of news or information is credible.

Think of it like buying a used car. You wouldn't go out to the nearest lot and buy the very first car you see, from the very first salesman you encounter. You'd shop around, maybe do a little research, and you certainly wouldn't accept everything the salesman said on its face. We should be out there applying the same scrutiny, the same healthy dose of skepticism to what we read, what we hear, what we share. We need to recognize that we're in a kind of information death spiral. We must take the time to consider the source, and to consider the new information we're taking in alongside the dissenting view. Bottom line: we ought to be reaching for reliable news outlets, with consistent track records of getting the story right—and knowledgeable analysts who take a thoughtful, measured approach to the news of the day and help to break it down for us.

Lately, I've had more people say to me "I don't know what to believe" than at any other time in my public life. They throw up their hands as if to say they're helpless against this cascading tide of information and misinformation. But we're not really all that helpless in this situation, when you think about it. In fact, we have enormous power in this regard. We have the power to dial down our reliance on social media. We have the power to switch the channel from time to time, and consider a different perspective. We have the power to think for ourselves and form our own opinions, instead of falling into lockstep with the pundit or politician who wants us to believe he or she is telling it like it is.

Here in this chapter, I'm calling on readers to exercise these powers—to get out of their silos and open their minds to the world around. And as long as I'm on it, I'll toss in a reminder that we shouldn't be so quick to write off our friends just because they have a different point of view. Lifelong friendships are hard enough to come by, so we'll do well to honor them by agreeing to disagree on certain issues.

On the heels of this information death spiral, more and more people are misinformed, while at the same time they've been given an ever-larger platform to speak their minds. That's a combustible mix, don't you think? To give people a greater voice when there's less and less merit to what they have to say, or less and less of a foundation on which they might build an argument?

This is not a criticism of the left or the right—it's just a new fact of life. Everyone's got a megaphone these days, which on its face is a great good thing, but before we start using those megaphones to call attention to an issue or a candidate or a cause we ought to know what we're talking about. Sadly, this is not always the case, because so many Americans are reaching for what I've taken to calling a reinforcing news media. They want to take in news and information that confirms what they think they already know. They want to use those megaphones to put their opinions on blast—opinions that have too often been shaped by only one side of the story.

One thing I want to make clear here: when I talk about reading and keeping informed, I'm not only talking about the news of the day. I'm talking about information in general because when we stop learning and *listening* to the world around us...that's when we stop growing as a society. The way we silo ourselves in terms of our news sources has its counterpart in the way we silo ourselves in terms of our relationships...*and* our interests. We tend to associate with people who agree with us, who already share a passion or concern...who *reinforce* what we already think and know. What we already *think* we know.

We're dug in, entrenched in a way that's not very interesting—a way that doesn't really allow us to move the conversation forward.

So what's the answer? Well, there's no *one* answer to set right the pendulum on this, but let me tell you what I do: I read. A lot. I listen to what people have to say—people I don't necessarily agree with, people I've never even heard about until I come across their names attached to a story that gets my attention. I try to keep an open mind, and when you read widely and listen attentively you're bound to pick up on a few things. For example, I like to read the science section of the *New York Times*. I find it very interesting. Just the other day, I came across an article on particle physics theory and learned all about the Higgs boson, which is sometimes called the "God Particle" and is believed to be the particle that gives mass to matter. I understood enough of what I read to find it fascinating, and I was eager to learn more, so when I found myself a week or so later talking to a physicist while on a tour of an imaging company, I started asking some questions. I wanted to know if it was true what people said about the Higgs boson being the missing atom that might disprove Einstein's theory of relativity. The guy nearly fell over—he didn't know what to make of me!

We need to stop demonizing people just because they support a candidate we oppose or stand on the opposite side of an issue—and those of us in politics need to stop demonizing people just because they stand on the opposite side of the aisle. A lot of my Republican friends think I've stepped away from my party when I try to defend Hillary Clinton. For whatever reason, they think she's terrible, but I push back on this. Secretary Clinton and I have had a cordial relationship over the years. She's been to my house. She's always been very nice to me. I don't agree with her on a lot of things, but that doesn't mean we can't come together on certain issues—like we did recently when we collaborated on an op-ed piece for the *Washington Post* on the illegal wildlife trade, following a move to drastically reduce appropriations for global conservation programs critical to the protection of wildlife and wild places.

"Although Congress has restored much of this critical funding in recent budget negotiations," we wrote, "the time has come to recognize that the world is less safe when criminals profit from stealing and poaching its wildlife and natural resources, and when shortages of fresh water, food, and other natural resources lead to instability and conflict."

Let us not forget that some of our boldest initiatives flow from the unlikely alliances that find us when folks find a way to come together from two decidedly different camps. A terrific illustration of this from my own experience is the compassion of Jesse Helms, the fire-breathing right-wing conservative senator from North Carolina who was so enormously helpful in getting debt relief for Africa, working in concert with Bono's ONE Campaign—a stirring example of someone the Democrats might have dismissed in their effort to bring humanitarian aid to people around the world simply because they didn't like some of the things he'd said or done on other issues.

I don't mean to sound the call for a national kumbaya moment. I'm not suggesting we all start holding hands and singing songs and glossing over our differences. But let's have some tolerance, people. Let's keep an open mind and make an extra effort to keep ourselves well-informed so that we can have a civil discussion on the issues that affect us.

Why in the world would we ever stop reading, listening, learning new things, exploring? Why would we refuse to listen to someone on an issue just because we happen to disagree with them on another issue? It makes no sense to me, and yet all over this country I'm afraid there are too many people who've become entrenched in their thinking. Worse, they've become complacent. They content themselves with what they already know and seem to have no desire to know anything more...or anything else.

You know, one of the most effective communication strategies I've developed over the years is to talk to people about something other than what we're meant to talk about. It's really not a strategy so much as an outgrowth of my personality. I like to talk to people, about pretty much anything. I like to listen to people, about pretty much anything. As long as they can find a way to make it interesting, I'm interested. I'll go to meet someone in their office, say, and I'll see a vacation photo on their desk, and I'll ask about where it was taken, what they enjoyed about their trip. I'll see a plaque or a medal from a marathon on the wall, and I'll ask about their running routine. It's telling to me, the things people put on display in their office, and when you ask them about these things it can help you to find some common ground, which is where we need to be if we hope to move this country forward—and, as a bonus, it warms people up and allows you to talk about whatever it is you're meant to talk about in a more collegial way.

So go ahead and shake things up. Read a book on a subject that's unfamiliar to you. Subscribe to a newspaper or magazine known for its in-depth reporting, one that doesn't rely on attention-grabbing, clickbait-type headlines to attract readers. Attend a lecture at your local college or university. And while you're shaking things up, be sure to mix things up, as well. If Fox News happens to be your thing, that's fine, but try to balance it out with a little bit of CNN. If you read the *Wall Street Journal*, take a look at the *New York Times*, as well.

Be discriminating in what you take in, so that what you put back out into the world is thoughtful, meaningful, impactful.

8

Put Yourself
In Someone Else's Shoes

We must learn to regard people less in the light of what they do or omit to do, and more in the light of what they suffer.

—Dietrich Bonhoeffer

Sometimes we need to look at the world through a lens other than our own. It's essential, really, and it goes deeper than simply reminding ourselves that some people have it harder than others, or that the things we might take for granted can be just out of reach for someone else.

In this chapter, I'll share the stories of two individuals who exemplify the spirit of empathy and compassion that can find us when we imagine what it's like to be in a difficult spot—the first, from the pages of history; the second, from the headlines of my local newspaper.

I'm betting most readers have never heard of Leopold Socha, a Polish sewer inspector from Lvov at the time of the Nazi occupation, even though they might know his story. Socha, a Catholic, helped to hide a group of twenty Jewish refugees during the Holocaust, using his vast knowledge of the city's sewer system to keep them from being discovered by German soldiers. The arrangement came about by accident. Socha discovered a group of these refugees on a routine examination of the canals beneath the Jewish ghetto, just prior to the final liquidation, and when it appeared that he would turn them in, they offered to pay him for his silence…and his expertise. And yet, what started out as a purely financial transaction became something far more consequential to Leopold Socha—and, ultimately, to the lives of the desperate men and women he'd taken into his safekeeping.

Together with his wife, Magdalena, and a fellow sewer worker named Stefan Wroblewski, Socha spent the next two months visiting the refugees on an almost daily basis. He would bring them food and water and medicine and clean clothes. His wife would take care of the laundry. Wroblewski would stand lookout on the streets above while Socha made his rounds, and when the refugees' hiding places were in danger of being discovered he would move them to a new location underground. The three of them did this at great risk to their own safety: if the Wehrmacht learned of their duplicity, they would have been shot and killed.

But then a curious thing happened. The Jewish refugees ran out of money. The leader of their group, a resourceful cabinetmaker named Ignacy Chiger, had pooled their money and sequestered it throughout the ghetto, together with their worldly possessions— jewelry, china, silverware, artwork. Each week, Chiger would tell Socha where he could find his next payment, and Socha would collect the bounty and share it with Wroblewski, according to their arrangement. And yet by the time the money ran out, Socha had begun to feel connected to this group of Jews, especially to Chiger and his family. On his visits, Socha would bring a little extra something special for Chiger's small children, Krystyna and Pawel, and he would sit with them and share a bite of his sandwich and read them stories, or walk them to a remote corner of the sewer where they could see a bit of sunlight so they would not lose hope.

So here's the curious part: instead of leaving Chiger and his fellow Jews to languish in the sewer without food or water or protection because they could no longer pay him, Socha offered to continue with his arrangement. However, he asked Chiger to keep up the charade of paying him each week, so that Socha in turn could keep paying Wroblewski—from the pile of money and loot he had already received as his share. It was, by almost every measure, a stunning and selfless reversal of roles, which came about because Socha had by this point begun to see himself in the plight of these desperate people. He could not abandon them to the sewers any more than he could betray his own family.

This arrangement continued for another year—fourteen months in all—and when the camps were finally liberated and the Nazis defeated, there were only ten Jewish refugees who'd survived the ordeal in the sewers.

In 1978, thirty-two years after his death, Socha was recognized by the State of Israel as one of the Righteous Among the Nations. There's a plaque in his honor at Yad Vashem, the World Holocaust Remembrance Center in Jerusalem.

I learned about Leopold Socha's story and came to cherish his example because Krystyna Chiger grew up to write a compelling memoir about her family's torment and triumph, *The Girl in the Green Sweater*, and because the story was eventually turned into a movie called *In Darkness*. What struck me in each account was the fearless compassion shown by this brave sewer worker. Yes, he might have been motivated by greed and opportunity at the outset, but after just a short time he developed such strong feelings for these good people that he could not turn his back on them, even if it meant giving back all the money and jewelry he'd already received and continuing to place his own life in jeopardy.

Their suffering was his suffering. Their hope was his hope. All because he had taken the time to step outside himself and his own circumstance to see the world through their eyes.

That's kind of what's happening in my hometown of Columbus, where Franklin County Municipal Court judge Paul Herbert presides over a pioneering initiative known as CATCH Court. The stakes are different for Judge Herbert than they were for Leopold Socha, but the lifeline he's holding out to a decidedly different group of desperate people is inspiring. In this case, CATCH stands for Changing Actions to Change Habits, and the way it works is Judge Herbert offers a second chance to local prostitutes who complete a two-year rehabilitation program. Like many judges and law enforcement officers, Judge Herbert was once inclined to look on prostitution as a kind of victimless crime that nevertheless needed to be prosecuted. His docket was filled with repeat offenders, who often struggled with drug and alcohol abuse—a drain on his little corner of our criminal justice system.

But as Judge Herbert started to see the same faces return to his courtroom over and over again, his heart opened up to these women. On those same faces he was also seeing despair, fear, uncertainty, and he tried to imagine how to fix what was broken in their lives, and in a system that was clearly not serving them. In many instances, the case files contained a trail of protection orders, and several of the women appeared before him with black eyes and bruises, bright red marks from choking, apparent burns. He began to look on them not as defendants but as victims of domestic violence and human trafficking, so he set about looking for ways to help break the cycle of abuse that kept sending them back into his courtroom.

In Ohio, as elsewhere, the scourge of human trafficking is a form of modern-day slavery. It's often unseen and yet everywhere apparent. In Franklin County, back in 2009 when CATCH Court was initiated, over 92 percent of women arrested for prostitution were identified as victims of human sex trafficking, initiated into this life at the average age of thirteen through force or coercion. Even women who managed to escape their circumstances continued to struggle with drug and alcohol abuse and home-lessness.

A lot of folks take the view Judge Herbert had when he first considered all of those prostitution cases, without stopping to think how these young women might have found themselves in such desperate cir-cumstances. No question, a vast number are driven into that life by cruel and abusive men—some after being abducted as young runaways and forced into prostitution by their captors. No question, before they become hardened to the ways of the street, these women are mistreated by their "boyfriends," their pimps, even members of their own family. Of course, there are some who become prostitutes for reasons having nothing to do with the many facets of human trafficking, but the pattern of abuse and neglect and hopelessness was a kind of through line in a lot of the stories Judge Herbert was hearing in his courtroom.

And so he thought to do something about it, setting up Franklin County's CATCH Court program as a kind of counterpoint to the "John Schools" you'll find in a lot of jurisdictions as part of the court-ordered penalty for solicitation. Here it was determined that the women who completed the two-year program would have their records expunged, making it easier for them to find meaningful employment. They'd also be given support services, like counseling and job training.

By almost every measure, the program has been an incredible success. As you might imagine, there is still a good deal of recidivism in Judge Herbert's courtroom, but following the first four years of CATCH Court there was a noted reduction in prostitution arrests—down from 1,745 in 2009 to 1,129 in 2013. Compellingly, there were no new arrests for 77 percent of CATCH Court graduates—meaning, once these women were given a second chance at life, most of them were able to find their footing.

A couple years into my term as governor, we started hosting the CATCH Court graduation ceremonies at the governor's mansion, and I found myself looking forward to the event each year for the way it reminded us how important it is to step outside ourselves and try to see a circumstance from the perspective of the person *in* that circumstance. Typically, each graduate would attend with friends and family members, and the day was always filled with hope and possibility and great good cheer, and I'd look on and think of the power to be found in hope and possibility and second chances—a power we might never find until we walk a couple hard miles in someone else's shoes.

The idea here is that we shouldn't be so quick to judge. When we take the time to visualize and perhaps even internalize the struggles and challenges facing others, we're better able to help them, to understand them, to support them. Sure, it's important to be resilient, as I wrote earlier, but sometimes a person simply can't see the sunrise. Sometimes a situation is so bleak there's no way out of it without a helping hand. Putting ourselves in someone else's shoes reminds us to be more compassionate, and more considerate, and it pushes us to a place where we can better appreciate our own blessings and think, There but for the Grace of God go I.

9

Spend Time Examining
Your Eternal Destiny

He that lives in sin, and looks for happiness hereafter,
is like him that soweth cockle and thinks to fill his
barn with wheat or barley.

—John Bunyan

As many readers might know, I am a man of faith. I have spent an adult lifetime studying some of history's great thinkers, trying to get at what it means to live a life of faith and purpose and meaning, and what's awaiting us as we move from the here and now into the great hereafter.

I've written about these issues, talked about these issues, prayed about these issues…and in so doing my faith has only deepened.

Here, let me tell you where I'm at with this:

I am a Christian.

I believe that our time on earth is guided by the values written on our hearts, not the values of this current age.

I believe God is love, forgiveness, grace, compassion, and unity.

I believe that our experiences in the here and now, and how we respond to these experiences, will shape our eternal souls.

There's been some debate about all of this, of course. Plato was one of the first philosophers to suggest that the soul goes on forever. Throughout history, people like St. Augustine, Thomas Aquinas, and Martin Luther shared some of these same views, and yet alongside this great and everlasting conversation on the meaning of life and man's ultimate destiny there's been a wide range of beliefs and not a whole lot of consensus.

One thing everybody seems to agree on, however, is that none of us is getting out of here alive. I hate to break it to you folks, but life is short. As much as we might want to argue the point, our days are numbered. And so I put it to you straight: What are you waiting for? What are you doing to make a difference? What is your legacy going to be?

Now, I'm not looking to get into the weeds on the issues of faith and religion. That's for a whole other book. In fact, I've written my own version of that whole other book—it's called *Every Other Monday*, and it's about the Bible study group that has sustained and enriched my life for the past thirty years. If you'd like to know more about my take on God and religion, I'd encourage you to read it. For the purposes of *this* book, however, I'm not going to bore you with my interpretation of Nietzsche or Aristotle or Kant, and I'm certainly not out to sell you on my beliefs. After all, we believe in our own ways. Or, not. We worship in our own ways. Or, not. That's for each of us to come to on our own. Or, not. But I'm guessing that if you've rolled up your sleeves and stayed with me to this point, there might be room in your open mind and open heart for a discussion on spirituality—or, at least, a meditation on how we ought to do right by each other and make some kind of difference while we're here.

By the way, I get so frustrated with preachers who engage in politics—that's one of the reasons a lot of folks are so down on organized religion these days. My feeling is, if you want to be in politics, take the collar off and run for office. And, of course, the inverse is also true: if you're a politician and you want to be a preacher, you ought to consider going to seminary.

When it comes to religion, we're all free to consider our eternal destinies in what ways we choose. All I'm asking is that you consider yours—really, that's all. I don't care if you've spent most of your life never even thinking

about matters of faith. Actually, that's not *entirely* true.
I do care—for your sake, not mine. I wholeheartedly
believe we all need to think about our spirituality, I do,
but maybe that's just not your thing. Maybe it's worked
out that you like to read the sports pages, or the fashion pages, or the stock tables. Maybe that's where your
interests lie. Maybe you're more of a concrete thinker
than an abstract thinker. Maybe you've been made to
feel uncomfortable by the trappings of organized religion and prefer to pray in your own way, or not at all.
Or maybe you've been so busy working like a dog in
order to make rent or put away some money for your
kids' college that you haven't had time to reflect on why
we're here. But what I want you to think about for the
next few moments is that we are indeed here, and that
we won't be here forever. I also want you to make room
in your thinking for the possibility that what we do during our lifetimes here on earth will somehow shape or
inform or even determine our lifetimes for all eternity.

Here again, I'm not asking you to accept this notion,
only to consider it. I mean, just because I believe in eternal life doesn't mean that you have to believe in eternal
life, but as long as I have your attention let me tell you
why I've come to this place in my thinking. Simply put,
it doesn't make sense to me that we're here on earth for

this short while and that's the end of it. People talk about it being some kind of leap of faith to live a life of faith, but I see it the other way—to me, it's a leap of faith *not* to believe. That idea doesn't correspond to what I read in scripture, or to what some of history's great minds have theorized about the meaning of life. You see, I happen to believe we have a creator. I happen to believe there is a God, and that He has given us the ability to distinguish right from wrong, and good from evil, and that if we live our life in the light of purpose and meaning we will be rewarded for it in the great beyond. We don't live in this way because we're hedging our bets and ticking off all the right boxes just so we might earn ourselves a place at the table in the world still to come, but because it's right and good and true—and it's this very righteousness and goodness and truth that will be rewarded.

If you were to sit down with an imam, a rabbi, a priest, and a minister and asked them to weigh in on what it means to have faith, to live a life of faith, and to look ahead to the life still to come, you'd likely be amazed at the similarities. You'd likely hear about humility and forgiveness, connectivity and hopefulness. You might even hear a discussion on the true meaning of the Arabic term *jihad*, which can probably best be described as a struggle with oneself, the constant striving to live a praiseworthy life in God's name and with God's guidance. You'd see that the underpinnings of the world's great religions are much the same, meant to help us place a clear set of guardrails around our lives and give us something to hold on to.

These guardrails are all-important. Just living our lives by what's in our hearts is not good enough, because our hearts don't always speak to us in the same ways. Human beings are capable of great good as well as great evil, so we must acknowledge that sometimes our hearts betray us, as we've seen throughout history. Indeed, we've had many wars over matters of faith and religion, but these conflicts come about when religion is distorted. In its purest form, faith in a higher power and belief in a guiding principle can provide restraint against the negative impulses that come with being human.

This puts me in mind of the lesson of *The Pilgrim's Progress*, one of the great religious allegories, written in the seventeenth century by a Puritan preacher named John Bunyan while he was imprisoned for conducting religious services without the authority of the Church of England. One of the themes of the book is man's determination to walk the path of righteousness, to get better and better, to move ever forward—in other words, to keep progressing toward the loftiest goal.

When you embrace this type of thinking and attach it to your worldview, it can be an enormously liberating thing. An uplifting thing. It can free us from the temptation to keep up with the Joneses, to chase these arbitrary markers we seem to set for ourselves to measure our successes in this life. The car, the promotion, the raise, the need to feel important…these things can weigh on us and add the kind of pressure to our days that can't help but distract us from our days. I'm not suggesting here that these things aren't important. We are meant to do well at our jobs, to work hard in school, to make good and full use of our talents. But the endgame is not meant to be the new car or the vacation home—no, we should think about chasing a higher reward.

I was reminded recently of the power to be found in living a life of purpose and meaning by a friend who had just gone to a funeral and told me of a poem that was read during the service that struck a resonant chord with him. The poem spoke of what it meant to live a life that reflects positively on your household. To make sure that all who meet you are somehow enriched. To pass each day in such a way that the many small kindnesses and sweet gestures you bestow on others will add immeasurably to the world around you as well as to your legacy. The great refrain of the poem was a call to live beneath "the crown of your good name"—calling to mind a phrase that first appears in the book of ethical teachings passed down to the rabbis in the time of Moses, where it is suggested that there are three crowns: the crown of Torah, or study; the crown of priesthood; and the crown of royalty. According to the teachings, to wear the crown—*any* crown—you needed to be born to it, or ascend to it through study and devotion. And yet there was also a fourth crown that was said to exceed the other three—the crown of a good name, through which we learn that a noble and enduring reputation is available to all who seek it and live with virtue.

This, to me, is what it means to live a life of faith, which these days looks a whole lot like what it means to live a life of humanity and compassion. They go hand in hand, and I hold them out here as a kind of paradigm because one of the things that gets under my skin about religion is how a lot of people think it's about the *don't*s instead of about the *do*s. Religion, for me, is not about our faults; it's about our potential. Religion, for me, is not about the downside; it's about the upside. Yes, it's about judgment of a kind, but it's a judgment combined immediately with grace. Maybe for you it's about something else, but this is my book, and you're here because you're curious about what I have to say, and what I have to say is this: without the moral compass that comes with the belief in a higher authority, we're nowhere. Without a belief in something bigger than ourselves, we'll never figure things out. I don't mean to suggest that the humanists among us are without a moral compass—far from it!—but I happen to believe that on a societal level there ought to be a commonly held belief in a higher power.

As long as I'm on it, I'll also say this: don't judge religion on the basis of what human beings do. We're all fallen. We're all flawed. But religion can provide us with a template to get it right. It can give us comfort, and perspective. If we allow it, it can give our lives meaning.

So let's go ahead and live a life bigger than ourselves, and let's start in on it straightaway. Let's remind ourselves each and every day that we know what it is to do the right thing, and then go ahead and do just that—because life is short. We can all agree with the great philosophers and theologians on this, and we should change our game plans accordingly. What do I mean by that? Well, I tell people all the time that they should live like they're in the middle of one of those two-minute drills at the end of a football game. You know how that goes, right? They play the game a certain way for fifty-eight minutes, and once the clock is against them they start throwing the ball all over the field and playing with a whole different energy. I've watched football my whole life, and I've never understood why teams don't play the game this way from the opening gun, but there's no denying the power that happens in those desperation pushes as time's running out. Sometimes, a team manages to turn things around and find a way to win. Sometimes, they just throw a last-minute scare into their opponents, maybe give them something to think about next time. But why not kick things up a notch from the very beginning? Or somewhere in the middle of the game? Why wait until the very last to give it your best shot when it's within you to give it your best shot all along?

I'm not suggesting here that we live with the kind of breathless urgency that comes at the end of a close football game. However, I do mean to sound a call to action. I do mean to put it out there that the time is now. These *ten little ways we can bring about big change* will only work if we set them in motion...so let's set them in motion.

You know, one of my goals in life is to work it out so that 70 percent of what people say about me when I die is true, but I'd never get to that number if I waited until there were two minutes left on the clock. I've lived by the values my parents instilled in me since I was a small child, and I mean to keep living by them. Sometimes, I stumble—*too often*, I stumble. But I know when I fall short that I must take the next opportunity to set things right, to live yet again in the light of these values. They've served me well so far, and if it works out that they will somehow carry me to the great hereafter…well, then, that'll be fine.

My point here, in keeping with the theme of this book, is that we would all do well to think about how we want to be remembered. So let's spend some time on this eternal destiny business and see how we might attach it to our days.

This is a hard concept for a lot of people. I get that. The idea that we will one day engage in joyful work in God's kingdom, and live in His glory…that there's a world still to come where there is no pain, no hatred, no sickness…it's just so hard to believe. It's almost like a fable. But I don't think of it that way. I've spent half my life in deep study on this, and what I can tell you is it's complicated. Religion is not about having blind faith and hoping for the best. It requires a lot of work, a lot of discipline. And in my case there's also been a healthy dose of skepticism because I would never have arrived at this place in my thinking had I not asked a lot of hard questions along the way.

So go ahead and ask your own hard questions. Do a deep dive and take a look at some of this stuff and see how it fits with the kind of person you are, the kind of person you've always *hoped* to become. Believe or don't believe, but why not live as if you do? Why not carry yourself with honor and dignity in expectation of some great reward? Not because there's some karmic quid pro quo at play. Religion doesn't work that way. Faith doesn't work that way. It's a little like loving your mother and father because you want to make sure you're in the will. You don't do right by your parents because you're angling for an inheritance. You do right by your parents because you love them, because you honor them, because you respect them. In the same way, we don't do right by each other because we're expecting some kind of bonus to come our way as a result. No, we do right by each other because we love each other. Because we're duty-bound to lift each other up, to celebrate each other, to care for each other.

Because it's the right thing to do.

10

Know That You Are
Made Special

Let us make our future now, and let us make our dreams tomorrow's reality.

—Malala Yousafzai

One of the greatest gifts we can give ourselves, and each other, is the reminder that we are all unique, so I want to end this volume by emphasizing the point: you are special, and you were made special, and you are meant to do something with *all* of your special gifts that no one else is able to do because they were not made in quite the same way.

That's a pretty awesome responsibility, don't you think? And so, for the final step in our ten-step approach to bringing about meaningful change, I'm asking readers to become the very best versions of themselves that they can be. To recognize that the Lord made them in this way for a reason, and that *it's up to us*—each of us!—to discover that reason and fulfill that purpose.

It's not such a big ask, really. After all, we're all part of the same puzzle. Our pieces are meant to fit together to create a beautiful mosaic that allows us to serve our communities and each other, and to make the world a better place. The difficulty comes in stepping back from our day-to-day and being painfully honest about how the choices we're making line up with the choices we are *meant* to make, and whether or not we're doing the most we can with what we've been given.

There's an old saying I used to hear all the time as a kid: "God don't make no junk." I'm not sure I love that line, but I offer it here for the way it signals that we are made with a purpose in mind—and for the way it reminds us to play our part in the orchestra. There's a reason we're here on this earth, and we ought to spend some time figuring out what that reason might be so we can find a way to honor it.

A lot of folks, they might be intimidated by this line of thinking, but I choose to find strength in the notion that there has never been someone exactly like me, and that there will never be another someone exactly like me. I know, I know… I'm setting myself up here for an easy line from my critics, who might be inclined to suggest that it's tough enough to have to deal with just *one* of me. But like it or not, like *me* or not, I'm unique…and so are you. And the thing of it is, it's up to each one of us to determine what it is we're meant to do with our special gifts.

I'm reminded here of the parable of the talents from the book of Matthew. It tells the story of a master who assigned the safekeeping of his gold to three servants. The first one took the gold and invested it aggressively, living a life a bit bigger than himself. The second one treated the gold more conservatively, being careful not to take too many risks. The third servant buried the gold in the ground because he didn't want to lose it, contenting himself with the status quo. When the master returned, he declared the third servant to be the "wicked" servant, and he gave all of his gold to the first servant, to reward him for using his "talents" to best advantage.

What I get from that story is the powerful (and empowering!) message that we are called upon to be the very best versions of ourselves. When you have a talent, you're meant to use it—to the fullest. If you don't, you're squandering your gifts. You're treading water, not serving anybody. The lesson, as I see it, is to take what you've been given and to build on it in such a way that it helps to make the world a better place. Anything less than that and you're just phoning it in.

During the 2016 campaign, I had a memorable exchange with a girl who'd come to one of my rallies. We were in St. George, Utah, in the southwestern part of the state—one of the most breathtakingly beautiful spots in the country. Really, the mesas and waterways down there are spectacular, and the people are spectacular as well—hardworking, God-fearing, life-affirming folks who seem to recognize how blessed they are to be able to live in the middle of such splendor. And here I spotted this teenage girl in the crowd and started talking to her, hoping to light an extra special something in her by sharing these ideas—and, in the process, hoping to get some of the other folks in the audience thinking in this way.

I said, "You know, there's never been anybody like you before and there will never be anyone like you again."

I told her she was special, and that she would find it in herself to leave a great legacy.

And do you want to know what happened? She started to cry. I wasn't looking to make her cry, of course. And I certainly wasn't expecting it. I was only out to give her some encouragement, maybe help her to realize how extraordinary she was, and that she was meant to do great things. But there she was, crying—trying *not* to cry, actually.

Afterward, I told Karen about it and she said, "John, you probably scared her."

Maybe I did, but I prefer to think I'd challenged this girl to think of her place in the world in a new way—a challenge I'd like to put out to everyone who's thought to pick up this book.

The message I find myself sharing when I travel the country talking to people—with *young* people especially, as I spend more and more time on college campuses—is that they shouldn't chase a paycheck, as they're casting about for a career or a course of study. In fact, that's a message I've taken in from *them*: the students I talk to are not particularly interested in how much money they can expect to earn on their first job; they're more interested in finding work that's meaningful, so I try to tell them that the two goals don't have to be mutually exclusive. They should be out there looking for something to do, something they're good at, that's rewarding in every sense. Granted, that's a luxury a great many Americans aren't quite able to afford, but when you're young and idealistic you're supposed to dream big, right? You're out to make the impossible seem possible. And so at the outset your chosen path should have as much to do with being fulfilled as getting paid. Sure, it'd be great if those two goals were in alignment, but that's not always the case. As my daughters were figuring out what they wanted to study in college, I put it to them the same way. I wanted them to know that it's not enough to want to be a doctor or a lawyer or a fashion industry executive if your only motivation is to draw a good living from your profession. That's only a small part of the deal. The bigger part is finding some way to tap those gifts that are uniquely yours, to chase a goal that fills your heart and brings you joy and allows you to be your very best self. The idea, therefore, is to match your dreams to your gifts, and in this way to discover your purpose while at the same time providing for your family and your future.

For a lot of us, our special purpose finds us away from work. We punch the clock and collect our paychecks, and then we go home and maybe live a life of service in our community, or devote ourselves to our children, or to an elderly family member. Our gifts are not always manifested in our careers—and in the goes-without-saying department, I want to stress that our salaries are never the true measure of our success or our accomplishments. And yet so many of us squander these gifts when we're scrambling to keep ahead of our bills.

I think back to a trip Karen and I took not too long ago. We were traveling with a young university student, and when we got to talking I asked this young woman what she was studying and what she hoped to do after college. I won't mention her field here because I don't want her to recognize herself in these pages and think I'm giving away a confidence, but I will say that her goals would have certainly set her up for a comfortable career. I thought, *Good for her.* But at the same time I also thought, *She can be doing so much more.* This particular young woman, she should have been reaching for something far bigger than just a comfortable career. So I said as much. I'm afraid it's not like me to hold my tongue over something like this, and I knew this young woman to be an exceptional student, with remarkable gifts, so I urged her to reach for something more...something *bigger.*

I said, "You're brilliant. You must push yourself into areas where you can put that brilliance to work."

The young woman thanked me, but I wasn't giving her a compliment, and I told her as much. I said, "Don't misunderstand, you didn't earn this brilliance. This was given to you. Don't think of it as a compliment but as a fact. Don't settle for a comfortable chair. You have to be uncomfortable."

I'm pretty sure this poor kid thought I was off my comfortable rocker, but I let her know my thinking on this, just as I am letting you readers in on the same. Fulfillment is the key—that's a message that applies to all of us, not just our young people. When you're fulfilled, that's when you find true satisfaction in life. When you're fulfilled, that's when you're in a position to help others. When you're fulfilled, that's when you have the bandwidth to consider the issues weighing on your community, your state, your country…and you're able to raise your hand and try to do something about them. When you're fulfilled, that's when you can develop the strength of character to lead, or to follow, or to weather the scrutiny that will surely come your way if you find yourself getting out in front on a cause or an issue.

To those who might wonder how they'll get to this place in their thinking or how they might find these opportunities that allow them to reach their full potential, I offer this: be patient. A lot of times, these opportunities will come to you, if you keep your head up and your eyes open to what's possible. And when they do, you'll know it in your heart that this was what you were meant to be doing all along.

Looking back on my own career and seeing where I am now, I like to think I'm fulfilled. Some days I feel this way in my bones. Others, I'm not so sure, so I keep striving, pushing, searching for the path I'm meant to follow. But I do know this: I've lived a fortunate life. I've had so many wonderful things happen to me—my parents could never have imagined the things I've been able to see and experience. Along the way, I've had the opportunity to meet and befriend people who've orbited Earth, people who've led nations, people who've led movements. Presidents, rock stars, dissidents, champions, missionaries...too many to list or even to count. And what I've come to recognize is that each one of them, at bottom, is just a person like you and me. They might have done great things and lived lives worth celebrating, but at one point they were just little kids on an uncertain path. They were like that girl in Utah, worried over the person she was meant to become, and yet they somehow found a way to fulfill their purpose, their dream, their vision.

I'm counting on you to do the same. Don't bury your talents or settle for that comfortable chair. Put yourself out there and make good things happen.

We're counting on you.

Closing Thoughts

It's Up to You

You must not lose faith in humanity. Humanity is like an ocean; if a few drops of the ocean are dirty, the ocean does not become dirty.

—Mahatma Gandhi

Here is my worry: we live in such frenetic times, it's impossible to predict the mood of the country in a week, in a month, in a year. The book you now hold in your hands is being written in the spring of 2019, against the backdrop of whatever frenzy is occupying our shared national attention at this moment.

It's a dizzying time, and it leaves me wondering what it must be like to live in Italy or Spain. From the outside looking in, it often appears to us that our European allies are out of sorts. Every few months, it seems, there's a change in government or a seismic shift in the public debate that would threaten our

American sensibility. We're used to things happening a certain way over here—or, at least, that's been the case until recently. Change has always tended to happen over time, in a small way, whereas in places like Italy and Spain they've tended to happen suddenly...*bigly*.

But that's gone out the window the past couple years, under our current administration. After centuries of apparent stability and decorum there's been a persistent whiplashing of the spirit on these shores, accompanied by a general upheaval to the workings of government. To judge from the headlines and the heated rhetoric that now seems to drive our social media, we're a country in chaos. What's down one day is up the next, and what strikes us at first blush as an outrage or an abomination very quickly becomes business as usual. It's amazing what we've gotten used to. It's like we've developed a kind of national thick skin that seems to mask who we really are underneath, and like many people I can't help but wonder how long we can keep this up.

Like I said, it's dizzying. And, wearying. If we let it, it can also be dispiriting, which takes me back to what's got me worried. If recent history is any barometer, it's reasonable to expect that from the moment I type these final few sentences until the moment of this book's publication there will be any number of controversies and bewilderments that might threaten to distract from the evergreen message at the heart of this volume. The field of Democratic hopefuls seeking the party's 2020 presidential nomination will have taken further shape—and, perhaps, a few Republican candidates might have emerged to challenge our incumbent president. The long fallout from the Mueller investigation will have changed our political landscape as well—and, tragically, there will no doubt have been mass shootings and global terror attacks and economic uncertainties and celebrity scandals that have commandeered our news cycles for a too-short while... until they will have been pushed from the front page by some other storm.

(God, I pray I'm wrong about all of this—and yet, I'm afraid, this is what our world has become.)

Underneath and alongside all of this uncertainty, you can bet, our president will have said something or done something to leave Democrats calling for his ouster, and Republicans reiterating their unflagging support, and those in the middle wondering how the heck we've gotten into this mess.

It's important to note here that the divisive, corrosive tone out of Washington is coming from both sides of the aisle. This is not a partisan issue. It's not even a political issue. The Democrats and Republicans are equally to blame. *We* are equally to blame—as a country, we have somehow been caught napping, our base instincts and self-interests momentarily out of alignment with our core values. There appears to have been a societal shift that now tells us our institutions and traditions are up for grabs, and that the decorum and civility we once expected from our elected officials (and, alarmingly, from each other) can no longer be taken for granted. We can't even count on too many of our leaders to tell us the truth. Just look at the "word of the year" choices for the past three years from the editors of our leading dictionaries: *post-truth* (*Oxford Dictionary*, 2016); *fake news* (*Collins Dictionary*, 2017); *misinformation* (Dictionary.com, 2018).

A lot of folks just don't know who or what to believe...or why the truth even matters.

This is what our world has become, and this is what's got me worried. Why? Because the disconnect we're facing is wider and louder and more troubling than I can recall, and yet it is my fervent hope that readers can find a way to dial down the uncertainty for long enough to consider some of the ideas in this book, because I believe they are important. Please know, these words have not been written in a vacuum—there's no such thing as a vacuum these days, with so much hot air coming out of Washington sucking up all the oxygen in the atmosphere. Know, too, that it's not just me seeking the anchor and succor I'm trying to offer in these pages. Since completing my second term as governor, I've been traveling the country giving speeches on how we might fix what's ailing America. Some of the issues I talk about are ripped from the day's headlines, while some are meant to remind us of the homespun values I believe we all share. What I'm hearing from audiences is that most Americans have had just about enough of the venom and vitriol that has lately passed for our national discourse, and that they're willing to hit the mute button on the nonsense and try on a new way of looking at our problems. There's a real call for sanity and calm. People are excited about the idea that the power to bring about true and lasting change resides in each of them, as individuals, and not just in our elected officials or our institutions.

You know, for the longest time, I thought I was done writing books. I've had a good run on the bookshelves—my last four books have been bestsellers, but it's becoming harder and harder to publish a book in today's media environment. I don't have the social media platform you need to really attract reader attention, and I didn't see the point in spending a whole lot of time writing a book if I couldn't get a whole lot of people to read it. But then something happened to change my thinking—actually, a couple things happened. The first found me on a brisk fall day, as I was winding down my second term as governor. I stopped to hit a few golf balls on my way to the gym because I'd been having some trouble with my swing. As I got myself set up at the driving range, I noticed a guy a few spots away from me who was hitting the ball really well, so I asked him to come over and maybe help me with my swing.

Apparently the guy knew me and wanted to make a little small talk, but I didn't have the head for small talk just then so I said, "Can we just do the chitchat later?"

(By the way, that's the side of me that people don't like. They tell me I'm brusque, short-tempered, impatient…and I suppose that's sometimes true. But I'm working on it—always, I'm working on it.)

Anyway, the guy gave me some pointers and when it felt to me like I'd taken up enough of his time I thanked him and said, "Okay, now we can chitchat. Tell me how we know each other."

So he told me. It turned out he was the nephew of

Rachel Muha, the mother of the Franciscan University student who'd been kidnapped and killed that I wrote about early on in these pages. Recall, Rachel was the woman who had it in her heart to forgive her son's killers and who was inspired to start a foundation in his memory to help keep "at risk" kids in her community from setting down a dark, desperate road.

At the time, this young man with the great golf swing had been so enraged by his cousin's death, he vowed revenge—and it was his anger, in large part, that pushed Rachel to compassion.

We talked for a while. It had been a couple years since his aunt had been celebrated by the Columbus Dispatch at a ceremony I'd been honored to attend, so I asked how she was doing and if he could put us back in touch.

And that was that...for the moment. But then, as I continued on to the gym, the second thing happened. I noticed a guy I'd seen there before. You know how those sightings go, right? When you're off doing your thing, and your routine runs into the routine of someone else doing his thing, and you nod or smile and continue on your way. On this day, though, I noticed my fellow gym rat's T-shirt, with a logo for an organization called The Miracle League. Something about the name struck me, so I asked him about it, and he told me about this tremendous group that makes it possible for children with disabilities to play baseball. The guy was really passionate about it and told me I should come by the field one day to see what these volunteers are able to do with these kids.

He said I should bring tissues because I'd be moved to tears.

We talked for a while, but when we returned to our workouts I got to thinking. It doesn't just happen that I run into these two shining examples of ordinary people doing extraordinary things in this back-to-back way. It doesn't just happen that you encounter two people connected to a real-life miracle. (One of them was basically announcing his miracle on his sleeve!) I thought it must be some kind of sign—from God, from the universe, from my literary agent…take your pick. Whatever it was, whatever it wasn't, I got to thinking it was on me to write a book about the good that people find a way to put out into the world, and along the way maybe take a look at how we might all be inspired to put out some of our own.

Jump ahead to where I am now, dotting the i's and crossing the t's on these pages. I'm not so full of myself to suggest that there's a hunger out there for the message I mean to deliver here, but I believe it's fair to call it a small appetite. If nothing else, I hope you'll at least consider these "little ways" as an encouraging course. Maybe take one or two of them to heart, and see if you start to look out at the world through a more hopeful lens, if the world begins to look back in kind. Maybe try them all on for size—taken together, they offer what I believe is the best hope for our future. Maybe borrow a page from the "nobodies" and "somebodies" and "everybodies" I've attempted to highlight here and start thinking about ways you can make your own kind of difference.

As I stated at the outset, we cannot rely on Washington to fix our problems for us. We cannot expect our elected officials to place our shared interests above their self-interests. We can only do what we can— be the change where we live and hope like crazy that everyone else starts doing the same.

Before you set this book aside, know this: I'm excited about the future of this country. I am. The best of America is yet to come. I know this in my bones to be true. I've seen what makes America work...what can make America *better*. I know that if you spend some time at your local food pantry, nobody's going to care a whit about your politics. I know that if you

show up on the Statehouse lawn to support sensible re-
strictions to our gun control laws that nobody's going
to call you out for being a traitor or an enemy of the
Second Amendment.

But it's on *you* to do all of these things. It's on *us*.
No one's going to sweep into town to save the day.
It's not going to happen. We have to solve our own
problems, and we can.

And we will.

And we must.

One of the things I realized that day I had those
back-to-back *miracle* encounters on the driving range
and at the gym was that writing a bestseller was an
arbitrary goal. The more meaningful goal, really, was
to move the needle in just one life, so that's what I've
set out to do—to write a book that could motivate just
one reader to make some kind of difference in their
own part of the world, in their own way.

So, tell me: Is that reader *you*?

★ ★ ★ ★ ★

Acknowledgments

One of my favorite aspects of this book-writing business is the chance it gives me to collaborate with so many thoughtful, mindful professionals. It takes many hands (and, many perspectives) to bring a book out into the world, and here I've been blessed to call on the talents of a number of individuals who have helped me to present my thoughts in just the right way.

I want to start by thanking my wife, Karen, for being so supportive of me in everything I do. Whenever I write a book, she's the first one to read over my shoulder and weigh in with a helpful, insightful comment. I also want to thank my daughters Reese and Emma, who sat through many a dinner table conversation as I talked through some of the ideas in this book—often adding some note and comment of their own.

Thanks to my friend and literary agent Jenny Bent of The Bent Agency, for setting this project in motion. I've worked with Jenny on all of my book projects, and she's been a tremendous ally and advocate. For the past several books, she's been helped along in this by her colleague John Silbersack, and I'm grateful to him as well.

Together, Jenny and John are responsible for introducing me to my friend and co-writer Dan Paisner—this is my fourth collaboration with Dan, who by this point has gotten pretty good at capturing my voice and helping me to shape and sharpen my ideas, so of course I also want to thank Dan for his friendship, and for his work in helping me to craft these pages and help me to make sure the tone was just right.

At Hanover Square Press, I've been fortunate to work with a team of publishing professionals who are passionate about the written word, and the positive changes that can come about on the back of just the right book, offered at just the right time, including our editor Peter Joseph, and his colleagues Natalie Hallak, Heather Connor, Laura Gianino, Mary Sheldon and Eden Church.

A number of friends kindly agreed to review the manuscript as it evolved, and I'm especially grateful to Beth Hansen, Bob Klaffky, Doug Preisse, John Weaver and Steve George for sharing their time, their thoughts, and their many helpful suggestions. My friends Craig MacDonald, Barney Skladany and Tom Barrett also rate a nod for their good counsel, as do my golf buddies who provide me with fellowship and the welcome distractions that help to make the game such a source of relaxation and release, including Dr. Michael Ports, Jack Tresoline, Randy Wilcox, Steve Casciani, John Minor, Bob Blair and Michael Thomas.

I also want to thank Trevor Johnson, who kept me organized and focused during this process, and Don Epstein, David Buchalter and the entire team at United Talent Agency, for helping me to share the message at the heart of this book with audiences all over the country.

A number of friends kindly agreed to review the manuscript as it evolved, and I'm especially grateful to Beth Hansen, Bob Klaffky, Doug Preisse, John Weaver and Steve George for sharing their time, their thoughts, and their many helpful suggestions. My friends Craig MacDonald, Barney Skladany and Tom Barrett also rate a nod for their good counsel, as do my golf buddies who provide me with fellowship and the welcome distractions that help to make the game such a source of relaxation and release, including Dr. Michael Ports, Jack Tresoline, Randy Wilcox, Steve Casciani, John Minor, Bob Blair and Michael Thomas.

I also want to thank Trevor Johnson, who kept me organized and focused during this process, and Don Epstein, David Buchalter and the entire team at United Talent Agency, for helping me to share the message at the heart of this book with audiences all over the country.